U.S. Department
of Transportation

**Federal Aviation
Administration**

M000086238

Airline Transport Pilot and Type Rating for Airplane

Airman Certification Standards

June 2019

**Flight Standards Service
Washington, DC 20591**

Acknowledgments

The U.S. Department of Transportation, Federal Aviation Administration (FAA), Office of Safety Standards, Regulatory Support Division, Airman Testing Branch, P.O. Box 25082, Oklahoma City, OK 73125 developed this Airman Certification Standards (ACS) document with the assistance of the aviation community. The FAA gratefully acknowledges the valuable support from the many individuals and organizations who contributed their time and expertise to assist in this endeavor.

Availability

This ACS is available for download at www.faa.gov. Please email comments regarding this document to afs630comments@faa.gov.

Material in FAA-S-ACS-11 will be effective June 28, 2019. All previous editions of the Airline Transport Pilot and Aircraft Type Rating Practical Test Standards for Airplane will be obsolete as of this date for airplane applicants.

Foreword

The Federal Aviation Administration (FAA) publishes the Airline Transport Pilot and Type Rating for Airplane Airman Certification Standards (ACS) document to communicate the aeronautical knowledge, risk management, and flight proficiency standards for airline transport pilot certification (ATP) and type rating certification in the airplane category and the following classes: single-engine land, single-engine sea, multiengine land and multiengine sea. This ACS incorporates and supersedes the previous Airline Transport Pilot and Aircraft Type Rating Practical Test Standards (PTS) for Airplane, FAA-S-8081-5.

The FAA views the ACS as the foundation of its transition to a more integrated and systematic approach to airman certification. The ACS is part of the safety management system (SMS) framework that the FAA uses to mitigate risks associated with airman certification training and testing. Specifically, the ACS, associated guidance, and test question components of the airman certification system are constructed around the four functional components of an SMS:

- Safety Policy that defines and describes aeronautical knowledge, flight proficiency, and risk management as integrated components of the airman certification system;

- Safety Risk Management processes through which internal and external stakeholders identify and evaluate regulatory changes, safety recommendations, or other factors that require modification of airman testing and training materials;

- Safety Assurance processes to ensure the prompt and appropriate incorporation of changes arising from new regulations and safety recommendations; and

- Safety Promotion in the form of ongoing engagement with both external stakeholders (e.g., the aviation training industry) and FAA policy divisions.

The FAA developed this ACS along with associated guidance and updated reference material in collaboration with a diverse group of aviation training experts. The goal is to drive a systematic approach to all components of the airman certification system, including knowledge test question development and conduct of the practical test. The FAA acknowledges and appreciates the many hours that these aviation experts have contributed toward this goal. This level of collaboration, a hallmark of a robust safety culture, strengthens and enhances aviation safety at every level of the airman certification system.

Rick Domingo
Executive Director, Flight Standards Service

Revision History

Document #	Description	Revision Date
FAA-S-8081-5F	Airline Transport Pilot and Aircraft Type Rating Practical Test Standards for Airplane	July 2008
FAA-S-ACS-11	Airline Transport Pilot and Type Rating for Airplane Airman Certification Standards	June 28, 2019

Table of Contents

Introduction

Airman Certification Standards Concept

The goal of the airman certification process is to ensure the applicant possesses the knowledge, ability to manage risks, and skill consistent with the privileges of the certificate or rating being exercised, in order to act as pilot-in-command (PIC).

In fulfilling its responsibilities for the airman certification process, the Federal Aviation Administration (FAA) Flight Standard Service (AFS) plans, develops, and maintains materials related to airman certification, training, and testing. These materials have included several components. The FAA knowledge test measures mastery of the aeronautical knowledge areas listed in Title 14 of the Code of Federal Regulations (14 CFR) part 61. Other materials, such as handbooks in the FAA-H-8083 series, provide guidance to applicants on aeronautical knowledge, risk management, and flight proficiency.

Safe operations in today's National Airspace System (NAS) require integration of aeronautical knowledge, risk management, and flight proficiency standards. To accomplish these goals, the FAA drew upon the expertise of organizations and individuals across the aviation and training community to develop the Airman Certification Standards (ACS). The ACS integrates the elements of knowledge, risk management, and skill listed in 14 CFR part 61 for each airman certificate or rating. It thus forms a more comprehensive standard for what an applicant must know, consider, and do for the safe conduct and successful completion of each Task to be tested on both the qualifying FAA knowledge test and the oral and flight portions of the practical test.

During the ground and flight portion of the practical test, the FAA expects evaluators to assess the applicant's mastery of the topic in accordance with the level of learning most appropriate for the specified Task. While the oral questioning will continue throughout the entire practical test, the evaluator must use discretion when asking questions during the flight portion of the evaluation and avoid distractions that could compromise safety of flight. For some topics, the evaluator will ask the applicant to describe or explain. For other items, the evaluator will assess the applicant's understanding by providing a scenario that requires the applicant to appropriately apply and/or correlate knowledge, experience, and information to the circumstances of the given scenario. The flight portion of the practical test requires the applicant to demonstrate knowledge, risk management, flight proficiency, and operational skill in accordance with the ACS.

Note: *As used in the ACS, an evaluator may be any person authorized to conduct airman testing under parts 61, 141, and 142 (e.g., an FAA aviation safety inspector (ASI), designated pilot examiner (DPE), or other individual authorized to conduct a test for a certificate or rating).*

Using the ACS

The ACS consists of **Areas of Operation** arranged in a logical sequence, beginning with Preflight Preparation and ending with Postflight Procedures. Each Area of Operation includes **Tasks** appropriate to that Area of Operation. Each Task begins with an **Objective** stating what the applicant should know, consider, and do. The ACS then lists the aeronautical knowledge, risk management, and skill elements relevant to the specific Task, along with the conditions and standards for acceptable performance. The ACS uses **Notes** to emphasize special considerations and refers the user to specific appendices concerning the conduct of the practical test. In particular, Appendix 7: Aircraft, Equipment, and Operational Requirements & Limitations contains additional information and evaluator considerations for many of the Tasks. The ACS uses the terms "will" and "must" to convey directive (mandatory) information. The term "may" denotes items that are recommended but not required. The **References** for each Task indicate the source material for Task elements. For example, in Tasks such as "Airport markings, signs, and lights." (AA.II.C.K3), the applicant must be prepared for questions on any airport markings, signs, and lights presented in the references for that Task.

The abbreviation(s) within parentheses immediately following a Task refer to the category and/or class aircraft appropriate to that Task. The meaning of each abbreviation is as follows.

> ATP: Initial issuance of an ATP Certificate only
> ASEL: Airplane – Single-Engine Land
> ASES: Airplane – Single-Engine Sea
> AMEL: Airplane – Multiengine Land
> AMES: Airplane – Multiengine Sea

Note: *When administering a test based on this ACS, the Tasks appropriate to the class airplane (ASEL, ASES, AMEL, or AMES) used for the test must be included in the plan of action. The absence of a class indicates the Task is for all classes. See Appendix 5: Practical Test Roles, Responsibilities, and Outcomes for all Task tables.*

Each Task in the ACS is coded according to a scheme that includes four elements. For example:

AA.I.B.K4:

    AA = Applicable ACS (Airline Transport Pilot – Airplane)
    I = Area of Operation I (Preflight Preparation)
    B = Task B (Performance & Limitations)
    K4 = Knowledge Task element 4 (Aerodynamics and how it relates to performance.)

Knowledge test questions correspond to the ACS codes, which will ultimately replace the system of Learning Statement Codes (LSC). After this transition occurs, the Airman Knowledge Test Report (AKTR) will list an ACS code that correlates to a specific Task element for a given Area of Operation and Task. Remedial instruction and re-testing will be specific, targeted, and based on specified learning criteria. Similarly, a Notice of Disapproval for the practical test will use the ACS codes to identify the deficient Task elements. Applicants and evaluators should interpret the codes using the ACS revision in effect on the date of the knowledge test.

However, for knowledge tests taken before this system comes on line, only the LSC code (e.g., "PLT058") will be displayed on the AKTR. The LSC codes link to references and broad subject areas. By contrast, each ACS code represents a unique Task element in the ACS. Because of this fundamental difference, there is no one-to-one correlation between Learning Statement (PLT) codes and ACS codes.

Because all active knowledge test questions for the Airline Transport Pilot Airplane Knowledge Tests now align with this ACS, evaluators can use LSC codes in conjunction with this ACS for targeting retesting of missed knowledge subject areas. The evaluator should look up the LSC code(s) on the applicant's AKTR in the Learning Statement Reference Guide available at:

https://www.faa.gov/training_testing/testing/media/LearningStatementReferenceGuide.pdf.

After noting the subject area(s), the evaluator can use the corresponding Area(s) of Operation and Task(s) in this ACS to narrow the scope of material for retesting to the appropriate ACS Area(s) of Operation and Task(s). Evaluators must verify the applicant has sufficient knowledge in those areas associated with incorrect responses on the knowledge test.

The applicant must pass the knowledge test before taking the practical test, if applicable to the certificate or rating sought. The practical test is conducted in accordance with the ACS and FAA regulations that are current as of the date of the test. Further, the applicant must pass the ground portion of the practical test before beginning the flight portion.

The FAA encourages applicants and instructors to use the ACS when preparing for the knowledge tests and practical tests. The FAA will revise the ACS as circumstances require. Evaluators conduct the practical test in accordance with the current ACS and FAA regulations. However, if an applicant is entitled to credit for Areas of Operation previously passed as indicated on a Notice of Disapproval or Letter of Discontinuance, evaluators should continue using the PTS/ACS effective on the test cycle start date.

I. Preflight Preparation

Task	A. Operation of Systems
References	14 CFR part 61; AC 90-117, AC 91.21-1, AC 91-78, AC 120-76; FAA-H-8083-2, FAA-H-8083-3, FAA-H-8083-23, FAA-H-8083-25; POH/AFM; Flight Standardization Board (FSB) Report (type specific)
Objective	To determine that the applicant exhibits satisfactory knowledge, risk management, and skills associated with airplane systems and their components; and their normal, abnormal, and emergency procedures. ***Note**: See Appendix 7: Aircraft, Equipment, and Operational Requirements & Limitations for information related to this Task.*
Knowledge	The applicant demonstrates an understanding of:
AA.I.A.K1	**Landing gear**—extension/retraction system(s), indicators, float devices, brakes, antiskid, tires, nose-wheel steering, and shock absorbers.
AA.I.A.K2	**Powerplant**—controls and indications, induction system, carburetor and fuel injection, turbocharging, cooling, mounting points, turbine wheels, compressors, deicing, anti-icing, and other related components.
AA.I.A.K3	**Propellers**—type, controls, feathering/unfeathering, auto-feather, negative torque sensing, synchronizing, synchrophasing, and thrust reverse including uncommanded reverse procedures.
AA.I.A.K4	**Fuel system**—capacity, drains, pumps, controls, indicators, cross-feeding, transferring, jettison, fuel grade, color and additives, fueling and defueling procedures, and fuel substitutions.
AA.I.A.K5	**Oil system**—capacity, allowable types of oil, quantities, and indicators.
AA.I.A.K6	**Hydraulic system**—capacity, pumps, pressure, reservoirs, allowable types of fluid, and regulators.
AA.I.A.K7	**Electrical system**—alternators, generators, batteries, circuit breakers and protection devices, controls, indicators, and external and auxiliary power sources and ratings.
AA.I.A.K8	**Pneumatic and environmental systems**—heating, cooling, ventilation, oxygen, pressurization, supply for ice protection systems, controls, indicators, and regulating devices.
AA.I.A.K9	**Avionics and communications**—autopilot, flight director, Electronic Flight Instrument Systems (EFIS), Flight Management System (FMS), Electronic Flight Bag (EFB), Radar, Inertial Navigation Systems (INS), Global Navigation Satellite System (GNSS), Space-Based Augmentation System (SBAS), Ground-Based Augmentation System (GBAS), ground-based navigation systems and components, transponder, Automatic Dependent Surveillance – Broadcast (ADS-B) In and Out, ADS – Contract (ADS-C), traffic awareness/warning/avoidance systems, terrain awareness/warning/alert systems, communication systems (e.g., data link, UHF/VHF/HF, satellite), Controller Pilot Data Link Communication (CPDLC), indicating devices, and emergency locator transmitter.
AA.I.A.K10	**Ice protection**—anti-ice, de-ice, pitot-static system protection, turbine inlet, propeller, windshield, airfoil surfaces, and other related components.
AA.I.A.K11	**Crewmember and passenger equipment**—oxygen system, survival gear, emergency exits, evacuation procedures and crew duties, quick donning oxygen mask for crewmembers, passenger oxygen system.
AA.I.A.K12	**Flight controls**—ailerons, elevator(s), rudder(s), control tabs, control boost/augmentation systems, flaps, spoilers, leading edge devices, speed brakes, stability augmentation system (e.g., yaw damper), and trim systems.
AA.I.A.K13	**Pitot-static system** with associated instruments and the power source for those flight instruments. Operation and power sources for other flight instruments.
AA.I.A.K14	**Fire & smoke detection, protection, and suppression**—powerplant, cargo and passenger compartments, lavatory, pneumatic and environmental, electrical/avionics, and batteries (on-aircraft and personal electronic devices).
AA.I.A.K15	**Envelope protection**—angle of attack warning and protection and speed protection.

I. Preflight Preparation

Task	A. *Operation of Systems*
AA.I.A.K16	The contents of the POH or AFM with regard to the systems and components in the airplane.
AA.I.A.K17	How to use a Minimum Equipment List (MEL) and a Configuration Deviation List (CDL).
Risk Management	The applicant demonstrates the ability to identify, assess, and mitigate risks, encompassing:
AA.I.A.R1	Failure to detect system malfunctions or failures.
AA.I.A.R2	Improper management of a system failure.
AA.I.A.R3	Failure to monitor and manage automated systems.
AA.I.A.R4	Failure to follow appropriate checklists or procedures.
Skills	For the airplane provided for the practical test, the applicant demonstrates the ability to:
AA.I.A.S1	Explain and describe the operation of the airplane systems and components using correct terminology.
AA.I.A.S2	Recall immediate action items or memory items, if appropriate.
AA.I.A.S3	Identify system or component limitations listed in the POH/AFM.
AA.I.A.S4	Demonstrate or describe, as appropriate, the process for deferring inoperative equipment (e.g., MEL) and using a CDL.
AA.I.A.S5	Comply with operations specifications, management specifications, and letters of authorization, if applicable.
AA.I.A.S6	Through the use of the appropriate checklists and normal and abnormal procedures, demonstrate the proper use of the airplane systems, subsystems, and devices, as determined by the evaluator.

I. Preflight Preparation

Task	B. Performance and Limitations
References	14 CFR parts 1, 61, and 91; AC 20-117, AC 61-138, AC 91-74, AC 91-79, AC 120-27, AC 120-58, AC 120-60, AC 135-17; FAA-H-8083-1, FAA-H-8083-2, FAA-H-8083-3, FAA-H-8083-23, FAA-H-8083-25; SAFO 19001; Chart Supplements; POH/AFM; AIM
Objective	To determine that the applicant exhibits satisfactory knowledge, risk management, and skills associated with operating an aircraft safely within its operating envelope. *Note*: See Appendix 7: Aircraft, Equipment, and Operational Requirements & Limitations for information related to this Task.
Knowledge	The applicant demonstrates understanding of:
AA.I.B.K1	Elements related to performance and limitations by explaining the use of charts, tables, and data to determine performance.
AA.I.B.K2	How to determine the following, as applicable to the class sought:
AA.I.B.K2a	a. Accelerate-stop / accelerate-go distance
AA.I.B.K2b	b. Takeoff performance (e.g., balance field length, V_{MCG})
AA.I.B.K2c	c. Climb performance
AA.I.B.K2d	d. Cruise performance (e.g., optimum and maximum operating altitudes)
AA.I.B.K2e	e. Descent performance
AA.I.B.K2f	f. Landing performance
AA.I.B.K2g	g. Performance with an inoperative powerplant for all phases of flight (AMEL, AMES)
AA.I.B.K2h	h. Weight and balance and how to shift weight
AA.I.B.K3	Factors affecting performance, to include:
AA.I.B.K3a	a. Atmospheric conditions
AA.I.B.K3b	b. Pilot technique
AA.I.B.K3c	c. Aircraft configuration (e.g., flap setting)
AA.I.B.K3d	d. Airport environment (e.g., runway condition, land and hold short operations (LAHSO))
AA.I.B.K3e	e. Loading (e.g., center of gravity)
AA.I.B.K3f	f. Weight and balance
AA.I.B.K4	Aerodynamics and how it relates to performance.
AA.I.B.K5	Adverse effects of exceeding an airplane limitation or the airplane operating envelope.
AA.I.B.K6	Effects of icing on performance.
AA.I.B.K7	Clean wing concept; deicing and anti-icing procedures to include use of appropriate de-ice fluid, hold-over tables, calculating hold-over times, and pre-takeoff contamination checks.
AA.I.B.K8	Air carrier weight and balance systems (e.g., average weight program). (ATP AMEL, AMES)
AA.I.B.K9	Runway assessment and condition reporting and use of the Runway Condition Assessment Matrix (RCAM). (ATP AMEL, AMES)
Risk Management	The applicant demonstrates the ability to identify, assess, and mitigate risks, encompassing:
AA.I.B.R1	Inaccurate use of performance charts, tables, and data.
AA.I.B.R2	Exceeding airplane limitations.
AA.I.B.R3	Possible differences between calculated performance and actual performance.
AA.I.B.R4	Airplane icing and its effect on performance and stall warning.
AA.I.B.R5	Runway excursions.
Skills	For the airplane provided for the practical test, the applicant demonstrates the ability to:
AA.I.B.S1	Describe the airspeeds used during specific phases of flight.
AA.I.B.S2	Describe the effects of meteorological conditions on performance for any phase of flight and correctly apply these factors to a specific chart, table, graph, or other performance data.
AA.I.B.S3	Describe the procedures for wing contamination recognition and any de-ice/anti-ice procedures prior to takeoff.

I. Preflight Preparation

Task	B. *Performance and Limitations*
AA.I.B.S4	Explain the adverse effects of airframe icing during all phases of flight. Describe any operating limitations for flight in icing conditions. If equipped, describe the procedures for de-icing and anti-icing system use and their effects on performance.
AA.I.B.S5	Compute weight and balance, including practical techniques to resolve out-of-limits calculations for a representative scenario, as specified by the evaluator.
AA.I.B.S6	Determine the computed center-of-gravity is within the acceptable limits and the lateral fuel balance is within limits for takeoff and landing.
AA.I.B.S7	Demonstrate proficient use of appropriate performance charts, tables, graphs, or other data to determine airplane performance and limitations for all phases of flight.

I. Preflight Preparation

Task	C. Weather Information (ATP)
References	14 CFR parts 61 and 91; AC 00-6, AC 00-30, AC 00-45, AC 00-54, AC 61-107, AC 61-138, AC 91-74; FAA-H-8083-16, FAA-H-8083-25; AIM
Objective	To determine that the applicant exhibits satisfactory knowledge, risk management, and skills associated with obtaining, understanding, and applying weather information for a flight under IFR. **Note:** See Appendix 7: Aircraft, Equipment, and Operational Requirements & Limitations for information related to this Task.
Knowledge	The applicant demonstrates understanding of:
AA.I.C.K1	Sources of weather data (e.g., National Weather Service, Flight Service) for flight planning purposes.
AA.I.C.K2	Acceptable weather products and resources utilized for preflight planning, current and forecast weather for departure and en route operations and arrival phases of flight.
AA.I.C.K3	Meteorology applicable to the departure, en route, alternate, and destination for flights conducted under Instrument Flight Rules (IFR) to include expected climate and hazardous conditions such as: **Note:** If K3 is selected, the evaluator must assess the applicant's knowledge of at least three of the following sub-elements.
AA.I.C.K3a	a. Atmospheric composition and stability
AA.I.C.K3b	b. Wind (e.g., crosswind, tailwind, windshear, mountain wave, etc.)
AA.I.C.K3c	c. Temperature
AA.I.C.K3d	d. Moisture/precipitation
AA.I.C.K3e	e. Weather system formation, including air masses and fronts
AA.I.C.K3f	f. Clouds
AA.I.C.K3g	g. Turbulence
AA.I.C.K3h	h. Thunderstorms and microbursts
AA.I.C.K3i	i. Icing and freezing level information
AA.I.C.K3j	j. Fog/mist
AA.I.C.K3k	k. Frost
AA.I.C.K3l	l. Obstructions to visibility (e.g., smoke, haze, volcanic ash, etc.)
AA.I.C.K4	Flight deck displays of digital weather and aeronautical information, their use to navigate around weather, and equipment limitations.
AA.I.C.K5	Low-visibility operations (e.g., surface movement, category II and III approaches). (ATP AMEL, AMES)
AA.I.C.K6	Flight Risk Assessment Tools.
Risk Management	The applicant demonstrates the ability to identify, assess, and mitigate risks, encompassing:
AA.I.C.R1	Weather conditions involved in departure and in-flight decision making, to include:
AA.I.C.R1a	a. Circumstances requiring a change in course or destination
AA.I.C.R1b	b. Known or forecast icing, winds or turbulence aloft, volcanic ash, destination weather, etc.
AA.I.C.R1c	c. Personal minimums
AA.I.C.R1d	d. Operator specified or aircraft operational limitations, if applicable
AA.I.C.R2	Limitations of:
AA.I.C.R2a	a. Onboard weather equipment
AA.I.C.R2b	b. Aviation weather reports and forecasts
AA.I.C.R2c	c. Inflight weather resources
Skills	The applicant demonstrates the ability to:
AA.I.C.S1	Interpret weather information, apply principles of aeronautical decision-making, and use a Flight Risk Assessment Tool, if available.

I. Preflight Preparation

Task	D. *High Altitude Aerodynamics (ATP) (AMEL, AMES)*
References	14 CFR part 61; AC 61-107, AC 61-138, AC 120-111; FAA-H-8083-3
Objective	To determine that the applicant exhibits satisfactory knowledge, risk management, and skills associated with high altitude airplane aerodynamics. **Note:** *See Appendix 7: Aircraft, Equipment, and Operational Requirements & Limitations for information related to this Task.*
Knowledge	The applicant demonstrates understanding of:
AA.I.D.K1	Aerodynamics of large transport category airplanes to include flight characteristics of swept wing airplanes (e.g., Mach buffet).
AA.I.D.K2	Energy management.
AA.I.D.K3	Relationship between Mach number, indicated airspeed, true airspeed, and change over altitudes.
AA.I.D.K4	Load factor at high altitude and its effect on high and low speed operating margins.
AA.I.D.K5	Relationship between altitude capability, weight, and temperature.
AA.I.D.K6	V_{MO}/M_{MO} convergence and stall angle of attack.
AA.I.D.K7	Maximum Lift over Drag Ratio (L/D Max).
AA.I.D.K8	Best range and best endurance.
AA.I.D.K9	Factors which contribute to airplane upsets at high altitude and upset prevention and recovery techniques.
Risk Management	The applicant demonstrates the ability to identify, assess, and mitigate risks, encompassing:
AA.I.D.R1	Failure to manage the airplane's energy state.
AA.I.D.R2	High operating altitudes at high operational weights.
AA.I.D.R3	High altitude slow-downs and excursions behind the power curve.
AA.I.D.R4	Turbulence at high altitude.
Skills	The applicant demonstrates the ability to:
AA.I.D.S1	If a cruise altitude is reached, manage the airplane's systems and energy state.

I. Preflight Preparation

Task	E. Air Carrier Operations (ATP) (AMEL, AMES)
References	14 CFR parts 25 and 121; AC 00-46, AC 61-138, AC 91.21-1, AC 91-78, AC 120-51, AC 120-66, AC 120-76, AC 120-82, AC 120-90, AC 120-101; AFM
Objective	To determine that the applicant exhibits satisfactory knowledge, risk management, and skills associated with air carrier operations. **Note:** See Appendix 7: Aircraft, Equipment, and Operational Requirements & Limitations for information related to this Task.
Knowledge	The applicant demonstrates understanding of:
AA.I.E.K1	Turbine engines, thrust reversing systems, and system malfunctions.
AA.I.E.K2	Airplane automation components (i.e., flight director, autopilot), their relationship to each other, and how to manage the automation for flight.
AA.I.E.K3	Advanced navigation equipment (e.g., FMS, RNP, ADS-B, EFB, etc.) and how it is used inflight.
AA.I.E.K4	Flightpath warning systems (e.g., TCAS, TAWS) and how to respond to a warning.
AA.I.E.K5	Altitudes and conditions that require the use of oxygen masks.
AA.I.E.K6	Causes and recognition of cabin pressure loss.
AA.I.E.K7	Appropriate rudder use in transport aircraft to avoid rudder reversal.
AA.I.E.K8	Crew communications (e.g., sterile flight deck rules, briefings).
AA.I.E.K9	Operational control.
AA.I.E.K10	Elements associated with operating at complex and high traffic airports with emphasis on runway incursion prevention techniques.
AA.I.E.K11	Professional responsibilities associated with being an ATP certificate holder and how to apply leadership skills as pilot in command.
AA.I.E.K12	Crew resource management (CRM) principles and application in a multi-crew environment.
AA.I.E.K13	Use of voluntary safety programs to manage risk across an organization (e.g., Threat and error management (TEM)).
AA.I.E.K14	Operations specifications.
Risk Management	The applicant demonstrates the ability to identify, assess, and mitigate risks, encompassing:
AA.I.E.R1	Turbine engine and thrust reversing system malfunctions.
AA.I.E.R2	Failure to manage automation and navigation equipment.
AA.I.E.R3	Failure to respond to a flightpath warning system alert.
AA.I.E.R4	Loss of cabin pressure.
AA.I.E.R5	Poor crew coordination.
Skills	The applicant demonstrates the ability to:
AA.I.E.S1	Apply CRM principles and use in a crew environment, as appropriate.

I. Preflight Preparation

Task	F. Human Factors (ATP)
References	14 CFR part 61; AC 61-107, AC 61-138, AC 120-51, AC 120-100; FAA-H-8083-2, FAA-H-8083-25; AIM
Objective	To determine that the applicant exhibits satisfactory knowledge, risk management, and skills associated with personal health, flight physiology, and aeromedical and human factors. **Note:** See Appendix 7: Aircraft, Equipment, and Operational Requirements & Limitations for information related to this Task.
Knowledge	The applicant demonstrates understanding of:
AA.I.F.K1	Causes, effects, recognition, and corrective actions associated with aeromedical and physiological issues including: **Note:** If K1 is selected, the evaluator must assess the applicant's knowledge of at least three of the following sub-elements.
AA.I.F.K1a	a. Hypoxia
AA.I.F.K1b	b. Hyperventilation
AA.I.F.K1c	c. Middle ear and sinus problems
AA.I.F.K1d	d. Spatial disorientation
AA.I.F.K1e	e. Motion sickness
AA.I.F.K1f	f. Carbon monoxide poisoning
AA.I.F.K1g	g. Stress
AA.I.F.K1h	h. Fatigue
AA.I.F.K1i	i. Dehydration and nutrition
AA.I.F.K1j	j. Hypothermia
AA.I.F.K1k	k. Optical illusions
AA.I.F.K1l	l. Dissolved nitrogen in the bloodstream after scuba dives
AA.I.F.K2	Effects of alcohol, drugs, and over-the-counter medications.
AA.I.F.K3	Aeronautical Decision-Making (ADM) using Crew Resource Management (CRM) or Single Pilot Resource Management (SRM), as appropriate.
AA.I.F.K4	Components of self-assessment for determining fitness for flight.
Risk Management	The applicant demonstrates the ability to identify, assess, and mitigate risks, encompassing:
AA.I.F.R1	Aeromedical and physiological issues.
AA.I.F.R2	Hazardous attitudes.
AA.I.F.R3	Distractions, loss of situational awareness, or improper task management.
Skills	The applicant demonstrates the ability to:
AA.I.F.S1	Perform a self-assessment and determine fitness for flight.

I. Preflight Preparation

Task	G. The Code of Federal Regulations (ATP)
References	14 CFR parts 61, 91, 117, 121, and 135; 49 CFR part 830
Objective	To determine that the applicant exhibits satisfactory knowledge of regulations applicable to the privileges and limitations of the ATP certificate and to flight operations that require an ATP certificate. **Note:** See Appendix 7: Aircraft, Equipment, and Operational Requirements & Limitations for information related to this Task.
Knowledge	The applicant demonstrates understanding of:
AA.I.G.K1	14 CFR part 61, subparts A, B, and G.
AA.I.G.K2	14 CFR part 91, subparts A, B, C, F, G, and H.
AA.I.G.K3	14 CFR part 117 (AMEL, AMES).
AA.I.G.K4	14 CFR part 121, subparts A, G, K, M, O, T, U, and V (AMEL, AMES).
AA.I.G.K5	14 CFR part 135, subparts A, B, C, D, E, F, and G (ASEL, ASES).
AA.I.G.K6	49 CFR part 830.
Risk Management	The applicant demonstrates the ability to identify, assess, and mitigate risks, encompassing:
AA.I.G.R1	Failure to comply with the applicable CFRs.
Skills	The applicant demonstrates the ability to:
AA.I.G.S1	Apply the CFRs to the flight/operation.

I.   Preflight Preparation

Task	H. *Water and Seaplane Characteristics, Seaplane Bases, Maritime Rules, and Aids to Marine Navigation (ASES, AMES)*
References	14 CFR part 61; FAA-H-8083-2, FAA-H-8083-3, FAA-H-8083-23; USCG Navigation Rules, International-Inland; POH/AFM; Chart Supplements; AIM
Objective	To determine that the applicant exhibits satisfactory knowledge, risk management, and skills associated with water and seaplane characteristics, seaplane bases, maritime rules, and aids to marine navigation.
Knowledge	The applicant demonstrates understanding of:
AA.I.H.K1	The characteristics of a water surface as affected by features, such as:
AA.I.H.K1a	a. Size and location
AA.I.H.K1b	b. Protected and unprotected areas
AA.I.H.K1c	c. Surface wind
AA.I.H.K1d	d. Direction and strength of water current
AA.I.H.K1e	e. Floating and partially submerged debris
AA.I.H.K1f	f. Sandbars, islands, and shoals
AA.I.H.K1g	g. Vessel traffic and wakes
AA.I.H.K1h	h. Other characteristics specific to the area
AA.I.H.K2	Float and hull construction and its effect on seaplane performance.
AA.I.H.K3	Causes of porpoising and skipping, and the pilot action needed to prevent or correct these occurrences.
AA.I.H.K4	How to locate and identify seaplane bases on charts or in directories.
AA.I.H.K5	Operating restrictions at various bases.
AA.I.H.K6	Right-of-way, steering, and sailing rules pertinent to seaplane operation.
AA.I.H.K7	Marine navigation aids, such as buoys, beacons, lights, sound signals, and range markers.
AA.I.H.K8	Naval vessel protection zones.
AA.I.H.K9	No wake zones.
Risk Management	The applicant demonstrates the ability to identify, assess, and mitigate risks, encompassing:
AA.I.H.R1	Local conditions.
AA.I.H.R2	Impact of marine traffic.
AA.I.H.R3	Failure to follow right-of-way and sailing rules pertinent to seaplane operations.
AA.I.H.R4	Limited services and assistance available at seaplane bases.
Skills	The applicant demonstrates the ability to:
AA.I.H.S1	Explain how float and hull construction can affect seaplane performance.
AA.I.H.S2	Describe how to correct for porpoising and skipping.
AA.I.H.S3	Locate seaplane bases on charts or in directories and identify any restrictions.
AA.I.H.S4	Identify marine navigation aids.
AA.I.H.S5	Describe what naval vessel protection zones and no wake zones are.
AA.I.H.S6	Assess the water surface characteristics for the proposed flight.
AA.I.H.S7	Perform correct right-of-way, steering, and sailing operations.

II. Preflight Procedures

Task	A. Preflight Assessment
References	14 CFR parts 43, 61, 63, 71, 91, 97, 117, 119, 121, and 135; AC 00-6, AC 120-27, AC 120-60, AC 135-17; FAA-H-8083-2, FAA-H-8083-3, FAA-H-8083-23, FAA-H-8083-25; POH/AFM; AIM
Objective	To determine that the applicant exhibits satisfactory knowledge, risk management, and skills associated with preparing for safe flight. **Note:** *See Appendix 7: Aircraft, Equipment, and Operational Requirements & Limitations for information related to this Task.*
Knowledge	The applicant demonstrates understanding of:
AA.II.A.K1	Pilot self-assessment.
AA.II.A.K2	Determining that the aircraft to be used is appropriate, airworthy, and in a condition for safe flight by locating and explaining related documents such as:
AA.II.A.K2a	a. Airworthiness and registration certificates
AA.II.A.K2b	b. Operating limitations, handbooks, and manuals
AA.II.A.K2c	c. Minimum Equipment List (MEL) and Configuration Deviation List (CDL)
AA.II.A.K2d	d. Weight and balance data
AA.II.A.K2e	e. Required inspections or tests and appropriate records and documentation (e.g., dispatch release) as applicable to the proposed flight or operation.
AA.II.A.K3	Preventive maintenance that can be performed by the pilot or other designated crewmember.
AA.II.A.K4	Aircraft preflight inspection including:
AA.II.A.K4a	a. Which items must be inspected
AA.II.A.K4b	b. The reasons for checking each item
AA.II.A.K4c	c. How to detect possible defects
AA.II.A.K4d	d. The associated regulations
AA.II.A.K5	Environmental factors including weather, terrain, route selection, and obstructions.
AA.II.A.K6	Requirements for current and appropriate navigation data.
AA.II.A.K7	Operations specifications, management specifications, or letters of authorization applying to a particular airplane and operation, if applicable.
Risk Management	The applicant demonstrates the ability to identify, assess, and mitigate risks, encompassing:
AA.II.A.R1	Human performance factors.
AA.II.A.R2	Inoperative equipment discovered prior to flight.
AA.II.A.R3	Environment (e.g., weather, airports, airspace, terrain, obstacles).
AA.II.A.R4	External pressures.
AA.II.A.R5	Aviation security concerns.
Skills	The applicant demonstrates the ability to:
AA.II.A.S1	Inspect the airplane in accordance with an appropriate checklist demonstrating proper operation of applicable airplane systems. Coordinate checklist with crew, if appropriate.
AA.II.A.S2	Coordinate with ground crew and ensures adequate clearance prior to moving doors, hatches, flight control surfaces, etc.
AA.II.A.S3	Document any discrepancies found; take corrective action and acknowledge limitations imposed by MEL/CDL items, if applicable.
AA.II.A.S4	Determine if the airplane is airworthy and in condition for safe flight.
AA.II.A.S5	Identify and comply with operations specifications as required.
AA.II.A.S6	Assess factors related to the environment (weather, airports, terrain, airspace).

II. Preflight Procedures

Task	A. Preflight Assessment
AA.II.A.S7	Ensure the airplane and surfaces are free of ice, snow, and frost. If icing conditions are present, demonstrates satisfactory knowledge of deicing procedures.

II.   Preflight Procedures

Task	B. Powerplant Start
References	14 CFR part 61; FAA-H-8083-2; POH/AFM; AIM
Objective	To determine that the applicant exhibits satisfactory knowledge, risk management, and skills associated with powerplant start procedures. ***Note:*** *See Appendix 7: Aircraft, Equipment, and Operational Requirements & Limitations for information related to this Task.*
Knowledge	The applicant demonstrates understanding of:
AA.II.B.K1	Normal and abnormal powerplant start procedures and limitations, including the use of an auxiliary power unit (APU) or external power source (if applicable).
AA.II.B.K2	Starting under various conditions.
AA.II.B.K3	Malfunctions during powerplant start, procedures to address the malfunction, and any associated limitations.
AA.II.B.K4	Coordinating and communicating with ground personnel for powerplant start, if applicable.
Risk Management	The applicant demonstrates the ability to identify, assess, and mitigate risks, encompassing:
AA.II.B.R1	Malfunctions during powerplant start.
AA.II.B.R2	Propeller and turbine powerplant safety.
AA.II.B.R3	Managing situations where specific instructions or checklist items are not published.
AA.II.B.R4	Personnel, vehicles, vessels, foreign object debris, and other aircraft in the vicinity during powerplant start.
Skills	The applicant demonstrates the ability to:
AA.II.B.S1	Ensure the ground safety procedures are followed during the before-start, start, and after-start phases.
AA.II.B.S2	Use appropriate ground crew personnel during the start procedures (if applicable).
AA.II.B.S3	Coordinate with crew, if applicable, and complete the appropriate checklist(s) prior to and after powerplant start.
AA.II.B.S4	Respond appropriately to an abnormal start or malfunction.

II. Preflight Procedures

Task	C. Taxiing (ASEL, AMEL)
References	14 CFR parts 61, 91, 121, and 135; AC 91-73, AC 120-57, AC 120-74; FAA-H-8083-2, FAA-H-8083-3, FAA-H-8083-25; POH/AFM; AIM; Chart Supplements; NOTAMs
Objective	To determine that the applicant exhibits satisfactory knowledge, risk management, and skills associated with safe taxi operations.
Knowledge	The applicant demonstrates understanding of:
AA.II.C.K1	Current airport aeronautical references and information resources such as the Chart Supplement, airport diagram, and NOTAMs.
AA.II.C.K2	Taxi instructions/clearances including published taxi routes.
AA.II.C.K3	Airport markings, signs, and lights.
AA.II.C.K4	Appropriate aircraft lighting for day and night operations.
AA.II.C.K5	Push-back procedures, if applicable.
AA.II.C.K6	Appropriate flight deck activities prior to taxi, including route planning, identifying the location of Hot Spots, and coordinating with crew if, applicable.
AA.II.C.K7	Communications at towered and nontowered airports.
AA.II.C.K8	Entering or crossing runways.
AA.II.C.K9	Night taxi operations.
AA.II.C.K10	Low visibility taxi operations and techniques used to avoid disorientation.
AA.II.C.K11	Single-engine taxi procedures (AMEL).
Risk Management	The applicant demonstrates the ability to identify, assess, and mitigate risks, encompassing:
AA.II.C.R1	Inappropriate activities and distractions.
AA.II.C.R2	Confirmation or expectation bias as related to taxi instructions.
AA.II.C.R3	A taxi route or departure runway change.
AA.II.C.R4	Failure to complete checklist(s).
AA.II.C.R5	Low visibility taxi operations.
Skills	The applicant demonstrates the ability to:
AA.II.C.S1	Record/receive taxi instructions, read back/acknowledge taxi clearances, and review taxi routes on the airport diagram.
AA.II.C.S2	Use an airport diagram or taxi chart during taxi.
AA.II.C.S3	Comply with ATC clearances and instructions and observe all runway hold lines, ILS critical areas, beacons, and other airport/taxiway markings and lighting.
AA.II.C.S4	Coordinate with crew, if applicable, and complete the appropriate checklist(s) prior to and during taxi, as appropriate.
AA.II.C.S5	Maintain situational awareness.
AA.II.C.S6	Maintain correct and positive airplane control, proper speed, appropriate use of wheel brakes and reverse thrust, and separation between other aircraft, vehicles, and persons to avoid an incursion/incident/accident.
AA.II.C.S7	Demonstrate taxi during day and night operations. If either condition is not available, the applicant must explain the differences between day and night taxi.
AA.II.C.S8	Demonstrate proper use of aircraft exterior lighting for day and night operations. If either condition is not available, the applicant must explain the differences between exterior aircraft lighting used for day and night operations.
AA.II.C.S9	Explain the hazards of low visibility taxi operations.

II. Preflight Procedures

Task	D. Taxiing and Sailing (ASES, AMES)
References	14 CFR parts 61, 91, 121, and 135; AC 91-73, AC 120-57, AC 120-74; FAA-H-8083-2, FAA-H-8083-3, FAA-H-8083-23, FAA-H-8083-25; POH/AFM; AIM; Chart Supplements
Objective	To determine that the applicant exhibits satisfactory knowledge, risk management, and skills associated with safe taxi and sailing operations.
Knowledge	The applicant demonstrates understanding of:
AA.II.D.K1	Current airport/seaplane base aeronautical references and information resources including Chart Supplements, airport diagram, and appropriate references.
AA.II.D.K2	Taxi instructions/clearances, if applicable.
AA.II.D.K3	Airport/seaplane base markings, signs, and lights.
AA.II.D.K4	Appropriate aircraft lighting for day and night operations.
AA.II.D.K5	Sailing elements and techniques and when sailing should be used.
AA.II.D.K6	Considerations for determining the most favorable sailing course.
AA.II.D.K7	Airport/seaplane base procedures including:
AA.II.D.K7a	a. Appropriate flight deck activities prior to taxi or sailing, including route planning, and coordinating with crew, if applicable
AA.II.D.K7b	b. Communications at towered and nontowered seaplane bases
AA.II.D.K7c	c. Entering or crossing runways (land operation)
AA.II.D.K7d	d. Night taxi and sailing operations
AA.II.D.K7e	e. Low visibility taxi and sailing operations
Risk Management	The applicant demonstrates the ability to identify, assess, and mitigate risks, encompassing:
AA.II.D.R1	Inappropriate activities and distractions.
AA.II.D.R2	Porpoising and skipping.
AA.II.D.R3	Failure to complete checklist(s).
AA.II.D.R4	Low visibility taxi and sailing operations.
AA.II.D.R5	Other aircraft, vessels, and hazards.
Skills	The applicant demonstrates the ability to:
AA.II.D.S1	Record/receive taxi instructions, read back/acknowledge taxi clearances, and review taxi routes on the airport diagram.
AA.II.D.S2	Use an appropriate chart during taxi, if published.
AA.II.D.S3	Comply with ATC clearances, as appropriate, and seaplane base/airport/taxiway markings, signals and signs.
AA.II.D.S4	Depart the dock/mooring buoy or ramp/beach in a safe manner, considering wind, current, traffic, and hazards.
AA.II.D.S5	Coordinate with crew, if applicable, and complete the appropriate checklist(s) prior to and during taxi or sailing, as appropriate.
AA.II.D.S6	Maintain sterile flight deck and situational awareness.
AA.II.D.S7	Maintain correct and positive airplane control, proper speed, appropriate use of reverse thrust, and separation between other aircraft, vehicles, vessels, and persons to avoid an incursion or right-of-way violation.
AA.II.D.S8	Position the flight controls, flaps, doors, water rudders, and power correctly for the existing conditions to follow the desired course while sailing and to prevent or correct for porpoising and skipping during step taxi.
AA.II.D.S9	Use the appropriate idle, plow, or step taxi technique.
AA.II.D.S10	Exhibit procedures for steering and maneuvering while maintaining proper situational awareness and desired orientation, path, and position.
AA.II.D.S11	Plan and follow the most favorable taxi or sailing course for current conditions.

II. Preflight Procedures

Task	D. Taxiing and Sailing (ASES, AMES)
AA.II.D.S12	Demonstrate taxi or sailing during day and night operations. If either condition is not available, the applicant must explain the differences between day and night taxi or sailing.
AA.II.D.S13	Demonstrate proper use of aircraft exterior lighting for day and night operations. If either condition is not available, the applicant must explain the differences between exterior aircraft lighting used for day and night operations.
AA.II.D.S14	Explain the hazards of low visibility taxi and sailing operations.

II. Preflight Procedures

Task	E. Before Takeoff Checks
References	FAA-H-8083-2, FAA-H-8083-3, FAA-H-8083-23, FAA-H-8083-25; POH/AFM
Objective	To determine that the applicant exhibits satisfactory knowledge, risk management, and skills associated with before takeoff checks. **Note:** *See Appendix 7: Aircraft, Equipment, and Operational Requirements & Limitations for information related to this Task.*
Knowledge	The applicant demonstrates understanding of:
AA.II.E.K1	Purpose of pre-takeoff checklist items including:
AA.II.E.K1a	a. Reasons for checking each item
AA.II.E.K1b	b. Detecting malfunctions
AA.II.E.K1c	c. Ensuring the airplane is in safe operating condition
AA.II.E.K2	Deicing and anti-icing procedures, holdover times, and pre-takeoff contamination check.
AA.II.E.K3	Adverse weather considerations for performance on takeoff (e.g., snow, ice, gusting crosswinds, low-visibility).
AA.II.E.K4	Items to be included in a before takeoff briefing.
Risk Management	The applicant demonstrates the ability to identify, assess, and mitigate risks, encompassing:
AA.II.E.R1	Division of attention while conducting before takeoff checks.
AA.II.E.R2	An unexpected change in the runway to be used for departure.
AA.II.E.R3	Failure to verify performance data is correct and airspeeds and flight instruments are set for actual conditions and the departure runway.
AA.II.E.R4	Failure to set navigation and communication equipment for departure.
AA.II.E.R5	Failure to configure autopilot and flight director controls for departure.
AA.II.E.R6	Failure to account for adverse weather conditions prior to takeoff (e.g., snow, ice, gusting crosswinds, low-visibility).
AA.II.E.R7	A powerplant failure during takeoff or other malfunction considering operational factors such as airplane characteristics, runway/takeoff path length, surface conditions, environmental conditions, and obstructions.
Skills	The applicant demonstrates the ability to:
AA.II.E.S1	Determine the airplane's takeoff performance for actual conditions and planned departure runway or waterway.
AA.II.E.S2	Coordinate with crew, if applicable, and complete the appropriate checklist(s) prior to takeoff in a timely manner.
AA.II.E.S3	Determine all systems checked are within an acceptable operating range and are safe for the proposed flight. During the checks, explain at the request of the evaluator, any system operating characteristic or limitation and any corrective action for a malfunction.
AA.II.E.S4	Determine airspeeds/V-speeds and set flight instruments appropriately, configure flight director, autopilot controls, and navigation and communication equipment for the current flight conditions and takeoff and departure clearances.
AA.II.E.S5	Conduct a briefing that includes procedures for emergency and abnormal situations (e.g., powerplant failure, windshear), which may be encountered during takeoff, and state the planned action if they were to occur.
AA.II.E.S6	Obtain and correctly interpret the takeoff and departure clearance.

III. Takeoffs and Landings

Task	A. Normal Takeoff and Climb
References	FAA-H-8083-2, FAA-H-8083-3, FAA-H-8083-23; POH/AFM
Objective	To determine that the applicant exhibits satisfactory knowledge, risk management and skills associated with a normal takeoff and climb. **Note:** *If a crosswind does not exist, the applicant's knowledge of crosswind elements must be evaluated through oral testing.* **Note:** *See Appendix 7: Aircraft, Equipment, and Operational Requirements & Limitations for information related to this Task.*
Knowledge	The applicant demonstrates understanding of:
AA.III.A.K1	Effects of atmospheric conditions, including wind, on takeoff and climb performance.
AA.III.A.K2	Appropriate V-speeds for takeoff and climb.
AA.III.A.K3	Appropriate aircraft configuration and power setting for takeoff and climb.
AA.III.A.K4	Runway markings and lighting.
Risk Management	The applicant demonstrates the ability to identify, assess, and mitigate risks, encompassing:
AA.III.A.R1	Selection of a runway, or runway intersection, based on pilot capability, aircraft limitations, available distance, surface conditions, and wind.
AA.III.A.R2	Wake turbulence.
AA.III.A.R3	Abnormal operations, to include planning for:
AA.III.A.R3a	a. Rejected takeoff
AA.III.A.R3b	b. Engine failure in takeoff/climb phase of flight
AA.III.A.R4	Improper aircraft configuration or settings (e.g., trim, flaps, autobrakes, etc.).
AA.III.A.R5	Collision hazards, to include aircraft, terrain, obstacles, wires, vehicles, vessels, persons, and wildlife.
AA.III.A.R6	Low altitude maneuvering including stall, spin, or CFIT.
AA.III.A.R7	Distractions, loss of situational awareness, or improper task management.
Skills	The applicant demonstrates the ability to:
AA.III.A.S1	Coordinate with crew, if applicable, and complete the appropriate checklist(s) prior to takeoff in a timely manner.
AA.III.A.S2	Make radio calls as appropriate.
AA.III.A.S3	Verify assigned/correct runway (ASEL, AMEL) or takeoff path (ASES, AMES).
AA.III.A.S4	Verify the airplane is configured for takeoff.
AA.III.A.S5	Position the flight controls for the existing wind.
AA.III.A.S6	Clear the area; taxi into takeoff position and align the airplane on the runway centerline (ASEL, AMEL) or takeoff path (ASES, AMES).
AA.III.A.S7	Retract the water rudders, as appropriate (ASES, AMES).
AA.III.A.S8	Establish and maintain the most efficient planing/liftoff attitude, and correct for porpoising or skipping (ASES, AMES).
AA.III.A.S9	Maintain centerline (ASEL, AMEL) and proper flight control inputs during the takeoff roll.
AA.III.A.S10	Confirm takeoff power and proper engine and flight instrument indications prior to rotation making callouts, as appropriate, for the airplane or per the operator's procedures.
AA.III.A.S11	Avoid excessive water spray on the propeller(s) (ASES, AMES).
AA.III.A.S12	Rotate and lift off at the recommended airspeed.
AA.III.A.S13	Establish a power setting and a pitch attitude to maintain the desired climb airspeed/V-speed, ±5 knots for each climb segment.

III. Takeoffs and Landings

Task	A. *Normal Takeoff and Climb*
AA.III.A.S14	Maintain desired heading ±5°.
AA.III.A.S15	Retract the landing gear and flaps in accordance with manufacturer or operator procedures and limitations, as appropriate.
AA.III.A.S16	Avoid wake turbulence, if applicable.
AA.III.A.S17	Follow noise abatement procedures, as practicable.
AA.III.A.S18	Complete appropriate after-takeoff checklist(s) in a timely manner.

III. Takeoffs and Landings

Task	B. Normal Approach and Landing
References	14 CFR part 61; FAA-H-8083-2, FAA-H-8083-3, FAA-H-8083-23; POH/AFM; AIM; SAFO 17010, SAFO 19001
Objective	To determine that the applicant exhibits satisfactory knowledge, risk management, and skills associated with a normal approach and landing. *Note: If a crosswind does not exist, the applicant's knowledge of crosswind elements must be evaluated through oral testing.* *Note: See Appendix 7: Aircraft, Equipment, and Operational Requirements & Limitations for information related to this Task.*
Knowledge	The applicant demonstrates understanding of:
AA.III.B.K1	A stabilized approach, to include energy management concepts.
AA.III.B.K2	Effects of atmospheric conditions, including wind, on approach and landing performance.
AA.III.B.K3	Wind correction techniques on approach and landing.
AA.III.B.K4	Runway markings and lighting.
Risk Management	The applicant demonstrates the ability to identify, assess, and mitigate risks, encompassing:
AA.III.B.R1	Selection of a runway or approach path and touchdown area based on pilot capability, aircraft limitations, available distance, surface conditions, and wind.
AA.III.B.R2	Wake turbulence.
AA.III.B.R3	Go-Around/Rejected Landing
AA.III.B.R4	Land and Hold Short Operations (LAHSO)
AA.III.B.R5	Collision hazards, to include aircraft, terrain, obstacles, wires, vehicles, vessels, persons, and wildlife.
AA.III.B.R6	Low altitude maneuvering including stall, spin, or CFIT.
AA.III.B.R7	Distractions, loss of situational awareness, incorrect airport surface approach and landing, or improper task management.
Skills	The applicant demonstrates the ability to:
AA.III.B.S1	Coordinate with crew, if applicable, and complete the appropriate checklist(s).
AA.III.B.S2	Make radio calls as appropriate.
AA.III.B.S3	Maintain a ground track that ensures the desired traffic pattern will be flown taking into consideration obstructions and ATC or evaluator instructions.
AA.III.B.S4	Ensure the airplane is aligned with the correct/assigned runway or landing surface.
AA.III.B.S5	Scan runway or landing surface and adjoining area for traffic and obstructions.
AA.III.B.S6	Select a suitable touchdown point considering wind, landing surface, and obstructions.
AA.III.B.S7	Establish the recommended approach and landing configuration and airspeed, ±5 knots, and adjust pitch attitude and power as required to maintain a stabilized approach.
AA.III.B.S8	Maintain directional control and appropriate crosswind correction throughout the approach and landing.
AA.III.B.S9	Make smooth, timely, and correct control application before, during, and after touchdown.
AA.III.B.S10	Touch down with the runway centerline between the main landing gear at the appropriate speed and pitch attitude at the runway aiming point markings -250/+500 feet, or where there are no runway markings 750 to 1,500 feet from the approach threshold of the runway. (ASEL, AMEL)
AA.III.B.S11	During round out and touchdown contact the water at the proper pitch attitude within 200 feet beyond a specified point (ASES, AMES). In addition, for AMES, the touchdown will be within the first one-third of the water landing area.
AA.III.B.S12	Decelerate to taxi speed (20 knots or less on dry pavement, 10 knots or less on contaminated pavement) to within the calculated landing distance plus 25% for the actual conditions with the runway centerline between the main landing gear. (At least one landing) (ASEL, AMEL)

III. Takeoffs and Landings

Task	B. Normal Approach and Landing
AA.III.B.S13	Use spoilers, prop reverse, thrust reverse, wheel brakes, and other drag/braking devices, as appropriate to safely slow the airplane. (At least one landing to a full stop)
AA.III.B.S14	Execute a timely go-around if the approach cannot be made within the tolerances specified above or for any other condition that may result in an unsafe approach or landing.
AA.III.B.S15	Utilize runway incursion avoidance procedures.

III. Takeoffs and Landings

Task	C. Glassy Water Takeoff and Climb (ASES, AMES)
References	FAA-H-8083-2, FAA-H-8083-23; POH/AFM
Objective	To determine that the applicant exhibits satisfactory knowledge, risk management, and skills associated with glassy water takeoff and climb. *Note: If a glassy water condition does not exist, the applicant must be evaluated by simulating the Task.* *Note: See Appendix 7: Aircraft, Equipment, and Operational Requirements & Limitations for information related to this Task.*
Knowledge	The applicant demonstrates understanding of:
AA.III.C.K1	Effects of atmospheric conditions, including wind, on takeoff and climb performance.
AA.III.C.K2	Appropriate power settings and V-speeds for takeoff and climb.
AA.III.C.K3	Appropriate airplane configuration.
AA.III.C.K4	Appropriate use of glassy water takeoff and climb technique.
Risk Management	The applicant demonstrates the ability to identify, assess, and mitigate risks, encompassing:
AA.III.C.R1	Selection of the takeoff path based on pilot capability, aircraft limitations, available distance, surface conditions, and wind.
AA.III.C.R2	Abnormal operations, to include planning for:
AA.III.C.R2a	a. Rejected takeoff
AA.III.C.R2b	b. Engine failure in takeoff/climb phase of flight
AA.III.C.R3	Collision hazards, to include aircraft, terrain, obstacles, wires, vehicles, vessels, persons, and wildlife.
AA.III.C.R4	Low altitude maneuvering including stall, spin, or CFIT.
AA.III.C.R5	Distractions, loss of situational awareness, or improper task management.
AA.III.C.R6	Failure to confirm gear position in an amphibious airplane.
Skills	The applicant demonstrates the ability to:
AA.III.C.S1	Coordinate with the crew, if applicable, and complete the appropriate checklist(s) prior to takeoff in a timely manner.
AA.III.C.S2	Make radio calls as appropriate.
AA.III.C.S3	Position the flight controls for the existing conditions.
AA.III.C.S4	Verify the airplane is configured for takeoff.
AA.III.C.S5	Clear the area; select appropriate takeoff path considering surface conditions and collision hazards.
AA.III.C.S6	Retract the water rudders, as appropriate.
AA.III.C.S7	Set and confirm takeoff power.
AA.III.C.S8	Avoid excessive water spray on the propeller(s).
AA.III.C.S9	Maintain directional control throughout takeoff and climb.
AA.III.C.S10	Establish and maintain an appropriate planing attitude, directional control, and correct for porpoising, skipping, and increase in water drag.
AA.III.C.S11	Utilize appropriate techniques to lift seaplane from the water considering the glassy water surface conditions.
AA.III.C.S12	Adjust power, as appropriate, and establish a pitch attitude to maintain the appropriate climb airspeed/V-speed, ±5 knots for each climb segment.
AA.III.C.S13	Retract flaps after a positive rate of climb has been verified or in accordance with manufacturer or operator procedures and limitations, as appropriate.
AA.III.C.S14	Follow noise abatement procedures, as practicable.

III. Takeoffs and Landings

Task	D. Glassy Water Approach and Landing (ASES, AMES)
References	FAA-H-8083-2, FAA-H-8083-23; POH/AFM
Objective	To determine that the applicant exhibits satisfactory knowledge, risk management, and skills associated with a glassy water approach and landing. **Note:** If a glassy water condition does not exist, the applicant must be evaluated by simulating the Task. **Note:** See Appendix 7: Aircraft, Equipment, and Operational Requirements & Limitations for information related to this Task.
Knowledge	The applicant demonstrates understanding of:
AA.III.D.K1	A stabilized approach, to include energy management concepts.
AA.III.D.K2	Effects of atmospheric conditions, including wind, on approach and landing performance.
AA.III.D.K3	Wind correction techniques on approach and landing.
AA.III.D.K4	When and why glassy water techniques are used.
AA.III.D.K5	How a glassy water approach and landing is executed.
Risk Management	The applicant demonstrates the ability to identify, assess, and mitigate risks, encompassing:
AA.III.D.R1	Selection of the approach path and touchdown area based on pilot capability, aircraft limitations, available distance, surface conditions, and wind.
AA.III.D.R2	Go-around/rejected landing.
AA.III.D.R3	Collision hazards, to include aircraft, terrain, obstacles, wires, vehicles, vessels, persons, and wildlife.
AA.III.D.R4	Low altitude maneuvering including stall, spin, or CFIT.
AA.III.D.R5	Distractions, loss of situational awareness, or improper task management.
AA.III.D.R6	Failure to confirm gear position in an amphibious aircraft.
Skills	The applicant demonstrates the ability to:
AA.III.D.S1	Coordinate with crew, if applicable, and complete the appropriate checklist(s).
AA.III.D.S2	Make radio calls as appropriate.
AA.III.D.S3	Ensure that the landing gear and water rudders are retracted, if applicable.
AA.III.D.S4	Consider the landing surface, visual attitude references, water depth, and collision hazards and select the proper approach and landing path.
AA.III.D.S5	Establish the recommended approach and landing configuration and airspeed, and adjust pitch attitude and power as required to maintain a stabilized approach.
AA.III.D.S6	Maintain a stabilized approach and recommended airspeed, ±5 knots.
AA.III.D.S7	Make smooth, timely, and correct power and control adjustments to maintain proper attitude and rate of descent to touchdown.
AA.III.D.S8	Maintain directional control throughout the approach and landing.
AA.III.D.S9	Contact the water in a proper pitch attitude and slow to idle taxi speed.

III. Takeoffs and Landings

Task	E. Rough Water Takeoff and Climb (ASES, AMES)
References	FAA-H-8083-2, FAA-H-8083-23; POH/AFM
Objective	To determine that the applicant exhibits satisfactory knowledge, risk management, and skills associated with a rough water takeoff and climb. **Note:** *If a rough water condition does not exist, the applicant must be evaluated by simulating the Task.* **Note:** *See Appendix 7: Aircraft, Equipment, and Operational Requirements & Limitations for information related to this Task.*
Knowledge	The applicant demonstrates understanding of:
AA.III.E.K1	Effects of atmospheric conditions, including wind, on takeoff and climb performance.
AA.III.E.K2	Appropriate power settings and V-speeds for takeoff and climb.
AA.III.E.K3	Appropriate airplane configuration.
AA.III.E.K4	Appropriate use of rough water takeoff and climb technique.
Risk Management	The applicant demonstrates the ability to identify, assess, and mitigate risks, encompassing:
AA.III.E.R1	Selection of the takeoff path based on pilot capability, aircraft limitations, available distance, surface conditions, and wind.
AA.III.E.R2	Abnormal operations, to include planning for:
AA.III.E.R2a	a. Rejected takeoff
AA.III.E.R2b	b. Engine failure in takeoff/climb phase of flight
AA.III.E.R3	Collision hazards, to include aircraft, terrain, obstacles, wires, vehicles, vessels, persons, and wildlife.
AA.III.E.R4	Low altitude maneuvering including stall, spin, or CFIT.
AA.III.E.R5	Distractions, loss of situational awareness, or improper task management.
AA.III.E.R6	Failure to confirm gear position in an amphibious airplane.
Skills	The applicant demonstrates the ability to:
AA.III.E.S1	Coordinate with crew, if applicable, and complete the appropriate checklist(s) prior to takeoff in a timely manner.
AA.III.E.S2	Make radio calls as appropriate.
AA.III.E.S3	Position the flight controls for the existing wind.
AA.III.E.S4	Verify the airplane is configured for takeoff.
AA.III.E.S5	Clear the area; select appropriate takeoff path considering surface conditions and collision hazards.
AA.III.E.S6	Retract the water rudders, as appropriate.
AA.III.E.S7	Set and confirm takeoff power.
AA.III.E.S8	Avoid excessive water spray on the propeller(s).
AA.III.E.S9	Maintain directional control and proper wind-drift correction throughout takeoff and climb.
AA.III.E.S10	Establish and maintain an appropriate planing attitude, directional control, and correct for porpoising, skipping, and increase in water drag.
AA.III.E.S11	Establish proper attitude and airspeed, lift off at minimum airspeed and accelerate to appropriate climb airspeed/V-speed, ±5 knots before leaving ground effect.
AA.III.E.S12	Retract the flaps after a positive rate of climb is established and a safe altitude has been achieved.
AA.III.E.S13	Maintain takeoff power to a safe maneuvering altitude then set climb power.
AA.III.E.S14	Follow noise abatement procedures, as practicable.

III. Takeoffs and Landings

Task	F. Rough Water Approach and Landing (ASES, AMES)
References	FAA-H-8083-2, FAA-H-8083-23; POH/AFM
Objective	To determine that the applicant exhibits satisfactory knowledge, risk management, and skills associated with a rough water approach and landing. **Note:** *If a rough water condition does not exist, the applicant must be evaluated by simulating the Task.* **Note:** *See Appendix 7: Aircraft, Equipment, and Operational Requirements & Limitations for information related to this Task.*
Knowledge	The applicant demonstrates understanding of:
AA.III.F.K1	A stabilized approach, to include energy management concepts.
AA.III.F.K2	Effects of atmospheric conditions, including wind, on approach and landing performance.
AA.III.F.K3	Wind correction techniques on approach and landing.
AA.III.F.K4	When and why rough water techniques are used.
AA.III.F.K5	How a rough water approach and landing is executed.
Risk Management	The applicant demonstrates the ability to identify, assess, and mitigate risks, encompassing:
AA.III.F.R1	Selection of the approach path and touchdown area based on pilot capability, airplane limitations, available distance, surface conditions, and wind.
AA.III.F.R2	Go-around/rejected landing.
AA.III.F.R3	Collision hazards, to include aircraft, terrain, obstacles, wires, vehicles, vessels, persons, and wildlife.
AA.III.F.R4	Low altitude maneuvering including stall, spin, or CFIT.
AA.III.F.R5	Distractions, loss of situational awareness, or improper task management.
AA.III.F.R6	Failure to confirm gear position in an amphibious airplane.
Skills	The applicant demonstrates the ability to:
AA.III.F.S1	Coordinate with crew, if applicable, and complete the appropriate checklist(s).
AA.III.F.S2	Make radio calls as appropriate.
AA.III.F.S3	Ensure that the landing gear and water rudders are retracted, if applicable.
AA.III.F.S4	Consider the landing surface, visual attitude references, water depth, and collision hazards and select the proper approach and landing path.
AA.III.F.S5	Establish the recommended approach and landing configuration and airspeed, and adjust pitch attitude and power as required to maintain a stabilized approach.
AA.III.F.S6	Maintain a stabilized approach and recommended airspeed with gust factor applied, ±5 knots.
AA.III.F.S7	Make smooth, timely, and correct power and control adjustments to maintain proper attitude and rate of descent to touchdown.
AA.III.F.S8	Contact the water at the correct pitch attitude and touchdown speed.
AA.III.F.S9	Make smooth, timely, and correct power and control application during the landing while remaining alert for a go-around should conditions be too rough.
AA.III.F.S10	Maintain positive after-landing control.

III. Takeoffs and Landings

Task	G. Confined-Area Takeoff and Maximum Performance Climb (ASES, AMES)
References	FAA-H-8083-2, FAA-H-8083-3, FAA-H-8083-23; POH/AFM
Objective	To determine that the applicant exhibits satisfactory knowledge, risk management, and skills associated with a confined area takeoff and maximum performance climb. *Note: See Appendix 7: Aircraft, Equipment, and Operational Requirements & Limitations for information related to this Task.*
Knowledge	The applicant demonstrates understanding of:
AA.III.G.K1	Effects of atmospheric conditions, including wind, on takeoff and climb performance.
AA.III.G.K2	Appropriate power settings and V-speeds for takeoff and climb.
AA.III.G.K3	Appropriate airplane configuration.
AA.III.G.K4	Effects of water surface.
AA.III.G.K5	Available techniques for confined-area takeoff and climb.
Risk Management	The applicant demonstrates the ability to identify, assess, and mitigate risks, encompassing:
AA.III.G.R1	Selection of the takeoff path based on pilot capability, airplane limitations, available distance, surface conditions, and wind.
AA.III.G.R2	Abnormal operations, to include planning for:
AA.III.G.R2a	a. Rejected takeoff
AA.III.G.R2b	b. Engine failure in takeoff/climb phase of flight
AA.III.G.R3	Collision hazards, to include aircraft, terrain, obstacles, wires, vehicles, vessels, persons, and wildlife.
AA.III.G.R4	Low altitude maneuvering including stall, spin, or CFIT.
AA.III.G.R5	Distractions, loss of situational awareness, or improper task management.
AA.III.G.R6	Failure to confirm gear position in an amphibious airplane.
Skills	The applicant demonstrates the ability to:
AA.III.G.S1	Coordinate with crew, if applicable, and complete the appropriate checklist(s) prior to takeoff in a timely manner.
AA.III.G.S2	Make radio calls as appropriate.
AA.III.G.S3	Position the flight controls for the existing wind.
AA.III.G.S4	Verify the airplane is configured for takeoff.
AA.III.G.S5	Clear the area; select appropriate takeoff path considering surface conditions and collision hazards.
AA.III.G.S6	Retract the water rudders, as appropriate.
AA.III.G.S7	Set and confirm takeoff power.
AA.III.G.S8	Avoid excessive water spray on the propeller(s).
AA.III.G.S9	Maintain directional control and proper wind-drift correction throughout takeoff and climb.
AA.III.G.S10	Establish and maintain an appropriate planing attitude, directional control, and correct for porpoising, skipping, and increase in water drag.
AA.III.G.S11	Rotate and liftoff at the appropriate airspeed, and accelerate to the recommended obstacle clearance airspeed or V_X using appropriate bank angles to maintain terrain clearance, as needed.
AA.III.G.S12	Climb at the recommended airspeed or in its absence at V_X, +5/-0 knots until the obstacle is cleared, or until the airplane is 50 feet above the surface. In multiengine airplanes with V_X values within 5 knots of V_{MC}, the use of V_Y or the manufacturer's recommendation is acceptable.
AA.III.G.S13	After clearing all obstacles, accelerate to V_Y ±5 knots.
AA.III.G.S14	Retract flaps and adjust power as needed to maintain V_Y or appropriate climb airspeed, ±5 knots to a safe maneuvering altitude.
AA.III.G.S15	Follow noise abatement procedures, as practicable.

III. Takeoffs and Landings

Task	H. Confined-Area Approach and Landing (ASES, AMES)
References	FAA-H-8083-2, FAA-H-8083-3, FAA-H-8083-23; POH/AFM
Objective	To determine that the applicant exhibits satisfactory knowledge, risk management, and skills associated with a confined area approach and landing. **Note:** See Appendix 7: Aircraft, Equipment, and Operational Requirements & Limitations for information related to this Task.
Knowledge	The applicant demonstrates understanding of:
AA.III.H.K1	A stabilized approach, to include energy management concepts.
AA.III.H.K2	Effects of atmospheric conditions, including wind, on approach and landing performance.
AA.III.H.K3	Available techniques for confined-area approach and landing.
AA.III.H.K4	Wind correction techniques on approach and landing.
Risk Management	The applicant demonstrates the ability to identify, assess, and mitigate risks, encompassing:
AA.III.H.R1	Selection of the approach path and touchdown area based on pilot capability, aircraft limitations, available distance, surface conditions, and wind.
AA.III.H.R2	Go-around/rejected landing.
AA.III.H.R3	Collision hazards, to include aircraft, terrain, obstacles, wires, vehicles, vessels, persons, and wildlife.
AA.III.H.R4	Low altitude maneuvering including stall, spin, or CFIT.
AA.III.H.R5	Distractions, loss of situational awareness, or improper task management.
AA.III.H.R6	Failure to confirm gear position in an amphibious aircraft.
AA.III.H.R7	Landing in an area or in conditions where a takeoff/climb may not be possible.
Skills	The applicant demonstrates the ability to:
AA.III.H.S1	Coordinate with crew, if applicable, and complete the appropriate checklist(s).
AA.III.H.S2	Make radio calls as appropriate.
AA.III.H.S3	Ensure that the landing gear and water rudders are retracted, if applicable.
AA.III.H.S4	Consider the landing surface, visual attitude references, water depth, and collision hazards and select the proper approach and landing path.
AA.III.H.S5	Establish the recommended approach and landing configuration and airspeed, and adjust pitch attitude and power as required to maintain a stabilized approach.
AA.III.H.S6	Maintain a stabilized approach and recommended airspeed with gust factor applied, ±5 knots.
AA.III.H.S7	Make smooth, timely, and correct power and control adjustments to maintain proper attitude and rate of descent to touchdown.
AA.III.H.S8	Touch down smoothly at the recommended airspeed and pitch attitude, beyond and within 100 feet of a specified point/area.
AA.III.H.S9	Maintain directional control and appropriate crosswind correction throughout the approach and landing.

III. Takeoffs and Landings

Task	I. Rejected Takeoff
References	FAA-H-8083-2, FAA-H-8083-3, FAA-H-8083-23; POH/AFM
Objective	To determine that the applicant exhibits satisfactory knowledge, risk management, and skills associated with a rejected takeoff. ***Note:*** *See Appendix 6: Safety of Flight and Appendix 7: Aircraft, Equipment, and Operational Requirements & Limitations for information related to this Task.*
Knowledge	The applicant demonstrates understanding of:
AA.III.I.K1	Conditions and situations that could warrant a rejected takeoff (e.g., takeoff warning systems, powerplant failure, other systems warning/failure).
AA.III.I.K2	Safety considerations following a rejected takeoff.
AA.III.I.K3	The procedure for accomplishing a rejected takeoff.
AA.III.I.K4	Accelerate/stop distance.
AA.III.I.K5	Relevant V-speeds for a rejected takeoff.
Risk Management	The applicant demonstrates the ability to identify, assess, and mitigate risks, encompassing:
AA.III.I.R1	Selection of the takeoff path based on pilot capability, aircraft limitations, available distance, surface conditions, and wind.
AA.III.I.R2	A powerplant failure or other malfunction during takeoff.
AA.III.I.R3	Failure to maintain directional control following a rejected takeoff.
AA.III.I.R4	A rejected takeoff with inadequate stopping distance.
AA.III.I.R5	A high-speed abort.
AA.III.I.R6	Distractions, loss of situational awareness, or improper task management.
Skills	The applicant demonstrates the ability to:
AA.III.I.S1	Abort the takeoff if the powerplant failure occurs prior to becoming airborne (ASEL, ASES).
AA.III.I.S2	Abort the takeoff if the powerplant failure occurs at a point during the takeoff where the abort procedure can be initiated and the airplane can be safely stopped on the remaining runway/waterway (AMEL, AMES).
AA.III.I.S3	Promptly reduce the power and maintain positive aircraft control using drag and braking devices, as appropriate, to come to a stop.
AA.III.I.S4	Coordinate with crew, if applicable, and complete the appropriate procedures, checklist(s), and radio calls following a rejected takeoff in a timely manner.

III. Takeoffs and Landings

Task	J. Go-Around/Rejected Landing
References	14 CFR part 61; FAA-H-8083-2, FAA-H-8083-3, FAA-H-8083-23; POH/AFM; AIM; FSB Report (type specific)
Objective	To determine that the applicant exhibits satisfactory knowledge, risk management, and skills associated with a go-around/rejected landing. ***Note:*** *See Appendix 7: Aircraft, Equipment, and Operational Requirements & Limitations for information related to this Task.*
Knowledge	The applicant demonstrates understanding of:
AA.III.J.K1	A stabilized approach, to include energy management concepts.
AA.III.J.K2	Effects of atmospheric conditions, including wind and density altitude on a go-around or rejected landing.
AA.III.J.K3	Wind correction techniques on takeoff/departure and approach/landing.
AA.III.J.K4	Situations and considerations on approach that could require a go-around/rejected landing, to include the inability to comply with a LAHSO clearance.
AA.III.J.K5	Go-around/rejected landing procedures, the importance of a timely decision, and appropriate airspeed/V-speeds for the maneuver.
Risk Management	The applicant demonstrates the ability to identify, assess, and mitigate risks, encompassing:
AA.III.J.R1	Delayed recognition of the need for a go-around/rejected landing.
AA.III.J.R2	Delayed performance of a go-around at low altitude.
AA.III.J.R3	Improper application of power.
AA.III.J.R4	Improper airplane configuration.
AA.III.J.R5	Collision hazards, to include aircraft, terrain, obstacles, wires vessels, vessels, persons, and wildlife.
AA.III.J.R6	Low altitude maneuvering including stall, spin, or CFIT.
AA.III.J.R7	Distractions, loss of situational awareness, or improper task management.
AA.III.J.R8	Managing a go-around/rejected landing after accepting a LAHSO clearance.
Skills	The applicant demonstrates the ability to:
AA.III.J.S1	Make a timely decision to go-around/reject the landing.
AA.III.J.S2	Apply the appropriate power setting for the flight condition and establish a pitch attitude necessary to obtain the desired performance.
AA.III.J.S3	Establish a positive rate of climb and the appropriate airspeed/V-speed, ±5 knots.
AA.III.J.S4	Configure and trim the airplane, when appropriate.
AA.III.J.S5	Make radio calls as appropriate.
AA.III.J.S6	Maintain the ground track, heading, or course appropriate for the conditions, or as specified by ATC or the evaluator.
AA.III.J.S7	Complete the appropriate procedures and checklist(s) in a timely manner.

IV. Inflight Maneuvers

Task	A. Steep Turns
References	FAA-H-8083-2, FAA-H-8083-3, FAA-H-8083-25; POH/AFM; FSB Report (type specific)
Objective	To determine that the applicant exhibits satisfactory knowledge, risk management, and skills associated with steep turns. **Note:** *See Appendix 7: Aircraft, Equipment, and Operational Requirements & Limitations for information related to this Task.*
Knowledge	The applicant demonstrates understanding of:
AA.IV.A.K1	Energy management concepts.
AA.IV.A.K2	Aerodynamics associated with steep turns, to include:
AA.IV.A.K2a	a. Coordinated and uncoordinated flight
AA.IV.A.K2b	b. Overbanking tendencies
AA.IV.A.K2c	c. Maneuvering speed, including the impact of weight changes
AA.IV.A.K2d	d. Load factor and accelerated stalls
AA.IV.A.K2e	e. Rate and radius of turn
Risk Management	The applicant demonstrates the ability to identify, assess, and mitigate risks, encompassing:
AA.IV.A.R1	Spatial disorientation when conducting a steep turn while flying by reference to instruments.
AA.IV.A.R2	Collision hazards, to include aircraft and terrain.
AA.IV.A.R3	Low altitude maneuvering including stall, spin, or CFIT.
AA.IV.A.R4	Distractions, loss of situational awareness, or improper task management.
AA.IV.A.R5	Failure to maintain coordinated flight.
Skills	The applicant demonstrates the ability to:
AA.IV.A.S1	Select an entry altitude that will allow the Task to be completed no lower than 3,000 feet AGL.
AA.IV.A.S2	Establish the manufacturer's recommended airspeed; or if one is not available, an airspeed not to exceed V_A.
AA.IV.A.S3	Establish at least a 45° bank solely by reference to instruments and make a coordinated steep turn of at least 180°, as specified by the evaluator.
AA.IV.A.S4	Perform the Task in the opposite direction, as specified by the evaluator.
AA.IV.A.S5	Make smooth pitch, bank, and power adjustments as needed.
AA.IV.A.S6	Maintain the entry altitude ±100 feet, airspeed ±10 knots, bank ±5°, and roll out on the specified heading, ±10°.
AA.IV.A.S7	Avoid any indication of an impending stall, abnormal flight attitude, or exceeding any structural or operating limitation during any part of the Task.

IV. Inflight Maneuvers

Task	B. *Recovery from Unusual Flight Attitudes*
References	14 CFR part 61; AC 120-111; FAA-H-8083-2, FAA-H-8083-15; POH/AFM; FSB Report (type specific)
Objective	To determine that the applicant exhibits satisfactory knowledge, risk management, and skills associated with recovering from unusual flight attitudes.
Knowledge	The applicant demonstrates understanding of:
AA.IV.B.K1	Procedures for recovery from unusual flight attitudes.
AA.IV.B.K2	Unusual flight attitude causal factors, including physiological factors, system and equipment failures, and environmental factors.
AA.IV.B.K3	The operating envelope and structural limitations for the airplane.
AA.IV.B.K4	Effects of engine location, wing design, and other specific design characteristics that could affect aircraft control during the recovery.
Risk Management	The applicant demonstrates the ability to identify, assess, and mitigate risks, encompassing:
AA.IV.B.R1	Situations that could lead to loss of control or unusual flight attitudes (e.g., stress, task saturation, and distractions).
AA.IV.B.R2	Failure to recognize an unusual flight attitude and follow the proper recover procedure.
AA.IV.B.R3	Exceeding the operating envelope during the recovery.
Skills	The applicant demonstrates the ability to:
AA.IV.B.S1	Use instrument cross-check and interpretation to identify an unusual attitude (including both nose-high and nose-low), and apply the appropriate pitch, bank, and power corrections, in the correct sequence, to return to a stabilized level flight attitude.

IV. Inflight Maneuvers

Task	C. Specific Flight Characteristics
References	14 CFR part 61; FAA-H-8083-2; POH/AFM; FSB Report (type specific)
Objective	To determine that the applicant exhibits satisfactory knowledge, risk management, and skills associated with flight and performance characteristics unique to a specific aircraft type. **Note:** See Appendix 7: Aircraft, Equipment, and Operational Requirements & Limitations for information related to this Task.
Knowledge	The applicant demonstrates understanding of:
AA.IV.C.K1	All specific flight and performance characteristics associated with the aircraft.
Risk Management	The applicant demonstrates the ability to identify, assess, and mitigate risks, encompassing:
AA.IV.C.R1	Specific flight and performance characteristics, their effects, and failure to follow procedures.
AA.IV.C.R2	Distractions, loss of situational awareness, or improper task management.
Skills	The applicant demonstrates the ability to:
AA.IV.C.S1	Use proper techniques, checklists, and procedures to enter into, operate within, and recover from specific flight situations, as applicable.

V. Stall Prevention

Task	A. *Partial Flap Configuration Stall Prevention*
References	AC 61-67, AC 120-109; FAA-H-8083-2, FAA-H-8083-3; POH/AFM; FSB Report (type specific)
Objective	To determine that the applicant exhibits satisfactory knowledge, risk management, and skills associated with stalls in a partial flap configuration. **Note:** *See Appendix 7: Aircraft, Equipment, and Operational Requirements & Limitations for information related to this Task.*
Knowledge	The applicant demonstrates understanding of:
AA.V.A.K1	Aerodynamics associated with stalls in a partial flap configuration, to include the relationship between angle of attack, airspeed, load factor, power setting, aircraft weight and balance, aircraft attitude, and sideslip effects.
AA.V.A.K2	Stall characteristics (i.e., airplane design) and impending stall and full stall indications (i.e., how to recognize by sight, sound, or feel).
AA.V.A.K3	Factors and situations that can lead to a stall during takeoff or while on approach and actions that can be taken to prevent it.
AA.V.A.K4	Effects of autoflight, flight envelope protection in normal and degraded modes, and unexpected disconnects of the autopilot or autothrottle/autothrust, if applicable to the aircraft used for the evaluation.
AA.V.A.K5	Fundamentals of stall recovery.
Risk Management	The applicant demonstrates the ability to identify, assess, and mitigate risks, encompassing:
AA.V.A.R1	Factors and situations that could lead to an inadvertent stall, spin, and loss of control during takeoff or while on approach.
AA.V.A.R2	Range and limitations of stall warning indicators (e.g., aircraft buffet, stall horn, stick shaker, etc.).
AA.V.A.R3	Failure to recognize and recover at the stall warning.
AA.V.A.R4	Improper stall recovery procedure.
AA.V.A.R5	Secondary stalls, accelerated stalls, elevator trim stalls, and cross-control stalls.
AA.V.A.R6	Effect of environmental elements on aircraft performance while in a partial flap configuration as it relates to stalls (e.g., turbulence, microbursts, and high-density altitude).
AA.V.A.R7	Collision hazards, to include aircraft and terrain.
AA.V.A.R8	Distractions, loss of situational awareness, or improper task management.
Skills	The applicant demonstrates the ability to:
AA.V.A.S1	Clear the area and select an entry altitude that will allow the recovery to be completed no lower than 3,000 feet AGL (non-transport category airplanes) or 5,000 feet AGL (transport category airplanes).
AA.V.A.S2	When accomplished in an FSTD, the entry should be consistent with the expected operational environment for a stall on takeoff or while on approach in a partial flap configuration with no minimum entry altitude defined.
AA.V.A.S3	Establish the takeoff or approach configuration (partial flap), as specified by the evaluator, and maintain coordinated flight in simulated or actual instrument conditions throughout the maneuver.
AA.V.A.S4	Either manually or with the autopilot engaged, smoothly adjust pitch attitude, bank angle (15°-30°), and power setting in accordance with evaluator's instructions to an impending stall.
AA.V.A.S5	Acknowledge the cue(s) and promptly recover at the first indication of an impending stall (e.g., buffet, stall horn, stick shaker, etc.).
AA.V.A.S6	Execute a stall recovery in accordance with procedures set forth in the POH/AFM.

V. Stall Prevention

Task	A. *Partial Flap Configuration Stall Prevention*
AA.V.A.S7	Retract the flaps or other lift/drag devices to the recommended setting, if applicable; retract the landing gear after a positive rate of climb is established, if applicable; and return to the desired flight path as specified by the evaluator.

V. Stall Prevention

Task	B. *Clean Configuration Stall Prevention*
References	AC 61-67, AC 120-109; FAA-H-8083-2, FAA-H-8083-3; POH/AFM; FSB Report (type specific)
Objective	To determine that the applicant exhibits satisfactory knowledge, risk management, and skills associated with stalls in a clean configuration. **Note:** *See Appendix 7: Aircraft, Equipment, and Operational Requirements & Limitations for information related to this Task.*
Knowledge	The applicant demonstrates understanding of:
AA.V.B.K1	Aerodynamics associated with stalls in a clean configuration, to include the relationship between angle of attack, airspeed, load factor, power setting, aircraft weight and balance, and aircraft attitude.
AA.V.B.K2	Stall characteristics (i.e., airplane design) and impending stall and full stall indications (i.e., how to recognize by sight, sound, or feel).
AA.V.B.K3	Factors and situations that can lead to a stall during cruise flight and actions that can be taken to prevent it.
AA.V.B.K4	Effects of autoflight, flight envelope protection in normal and degraded modes, and unexpected disconnects of the autopilot or autothrottle/autothrust, if applicable to the aircraft used for the evaluation.
AA.V.B.K5	Fundamentals of stall recovery.
AA.V.B.K6	Effects of altitude on performance (e.g., thrust available) and flight control effectiveness during a recovery.
Risk Management	The applicant demonstrates the ability to identify, assess, and mitigate risks, encompassing:
AA.V.B.R1	Factors and situations that could lead to an inadvertent stall, spin, and loss of control during cruise flight.
AA.V.B.R2	Range and limitations of stall warning indicators (e.g., aircraft buffet, stall horn, stick shaker, etc.).
AA.V.B.R3	Failure to recognize and recover at the stall warning.
AA.V.B.R4	Improper stall recovery procedure.
AA.V.B.R5	Secondary stalls, accelerated stalls, elevator trim stalls, and cross-control stalls.
AA.V.B.R6	Effect of environmental elements on aircraft performance while in cruise flight as it relates to stalls (e.g., turbulence, microbursts, and high-density altitude).
AA.V.B.R7	Collision hazards, to include aircraft and terrain.
AA.V.B.R8	Distractions, loss of situational awareness, or improper task management.
Skills	The applicant demonstrates the ability to:
AA.V.B.S1	Clear the area and select an entry altitude that will allow the recovery to be completed no lower than 3,000 feet AGL (non-transport category airplanes) or 5,000 feet AGL (transport category airplanes).
AA.V.B.S2	When accomplished in an FSTD, the entry should be consistent with the expected operational environment for a stall in cruise flight with no minimum entry altitude defined.
AA.V.B.S3	While in cruise flight, maintain coordinated flight in simulated or actual instrument conditions throughout the maneuver.
AA.V.B.S4	Either manually or with the autopilot engaged, smoothly adjust pitch attitude, bank angle (15°-30°), and power setting in accordance with evaluator's instructions to an impending stall.
AA.V.B.S5	Acknowledge the cue(s) and promptly recover at the first indication of an impending stall (e.g., buffet, stall horn, stick shaker, etc.).
AA.V.B.S6	Execute a stall recovery in accordance with procedures set forth in the POH/AFM.
AA.V.B.S7	Return to the desired flight path as specified by the evaluator.

V. Stall Prevention

Task	C. Landing Configuration Stall Prevention
References	AC 61-67, AC 120-109; FAA-H-8083-2, FAA-H-8083-3; POH/AFM; FSB Report (type specific)
Objective	To determine that the applicant exhibits satisfactory knowledge, risk management, and skills associated with stalls in the landing configuration. **Note:** *See Appendix 7: Aircraft, Equipment, and Operational Requirements & Limitations for information related to this Task.*
Knowledge	The applicant demonstrates understanding of:
AA.V.C.K1	Aerodynamics associated with stalls in the landing configuration, to include the relationship between angle of attack, airspeed, load factor, power setting, aircraft weight and balance, aircraft attitude, and sideslip effects.
AA.V.C.K2	Stall characteristics (i.e., airplane design) and impending stall and full stall indications (i.e., how to recognize by sight, sound, or feel).
AA.V.C.K3	Factors and situations that can lead to a stall when configured for landing and actions that can be taken to prevent it.
AA.V.C.K4	Effects of autoflight, flight envelope protection in normal and degraded modes, and unexpected disconnects of the autopilot or autothrottle/autothrust, if applicable to the aircraft used for the evaluation.
AA.V.C.K5	Fundamentals of stall recovery.
Risk Management	The applicant demonstrates the ability to identify, assess, and mitigate risks, encompassing:
AA.V.C.R1	Factors and situations that could lead to an inadvertent stall, spin, and loss of control during landing.
AA.V.C.R2	Range and limitations of stall warning indicators (e.g., aircraft buffet, stall horn, stick shaker, etc.).
AA.V.C.R3	Failure to recognize and recover at the stall warning.
AA.V.C.R4	Improper stall recovery procedure.
AA.V.C.R5	Secondary stalls, accelerated stalls, elevator trim stalls, and cross-control stalls.
AA.V.C.R6	Effect of environmental elements on aircraft performance while landing as it relates to stalls (e.g., turbulence, icing, microbursts, and high-density altitude).
AA.V.C.R7	Stalls at a low altitude.
AA.V.C.R8	Collision hazards, to include aircraft and terrain.
AA.V.C.R9	Distractions, loss of situational awareness, or improper task management.
Skills	The applicant demonstrates the ability to:
AA.V.C.S1	Clear the area and select an entry altitude that will allow the recovery to be completed no lower than 3,000 feet AGL (non-transport category airplanes) or 5,000 feet AGL (transport category airplanes).
AA.V.C.S2	When accomplished in an FSTD, the entry should be consistent with the expected operational environment for a stall when fully configured for landing with no minimum entry altitude defined.
AA.V.C.S3	Establish the landing configuration (i.e., lift/drag devices set and landing gear extended) and maintain coordinated flight in simulated or actual instrument conditions throughout the maneuver.
AA.V.C.S4	Either manually or with the autopilot engaged, smoothly adjust pitch attitude, bank angle (15°-30°), and power setting in accordance with evaluator's instructions to an impending stall.
AA.V.C.S5	Acknowledge the cue(s) and promptly recover at the first indication of an impending stall (e.g., buffet, stall horn, stick shaker, etc.).
AA.V.C.S6	Execute a stall recovery in accordance with procedures set forth in the POH/AFM.

V. Stall Prevention

Task	C. Landing Configuration Stall Prevention
AA.V.C.S7	Retract the flaps or other lift/drag devices to the recommended setting, if applicable; retract the landing gear after a positive rate of climb is established, if applicable; and return to the desired flight path as specified by the evaluator.

VI. Instrument Procedures

Task	A. Instrument Takeoff
References	14 CFR parts 61 and 91; FAA-H-8083-2, FAA-H-8083-3, FAA-H-8083-6, FAA-H-8083-15, FAA-H-8083-16, FAA-H-8083-23, FAA-H-8083-25; POH/AFM; AIM; TPP
Objective	To determine that the applicant exhibits satisfactory knowledge, risk management, and skills associated with an instrument takeoff. *Note: See Appendix 7: Aircraft, Equipment, and Operational Requirements & Limitations for information related to this Task.*
Knowledge	The applicant demonstrates understanding of:
AA.VI.A.K1	Operational factors that could affect an instrument takeoff (e.g., runway length, runway lighting, surface conditions, wind, wake turbulence, icing conditions, obstructions, available instrument approaches or alternate airports available in the event of an emergency after takeoff).
Risk Management	The applicant demonstrates the ability to identify, assess, and mitigate risks, encompassing:
AA.VI.A.R1	Selection of a runway based on pilot capability, aircraft performance and limitations, available distance, surface conditions, lighting, and wind.
AA.VI.A.R2	Wake turbulence.
AA.VI.A.R3	Abnormal operations, to include planning for:
AA.VI.A.R3a	a. Rejected takeoff
AA.VI.A.R3b	b. Engine failure in takeoff/climb phase of flight with the ceiling or visibility below the minimums for an instrument approach at departure airport
AA.VI.A.R4	Collision hazards, to include aircraft, terrain, obstacles, wires, vehicles, vessels, persons, and wildlife.
AA.VI.A.R5	Low altitude maneuvering including stall, spin, or CFIT.
AA.VI.A.R6	Distractions, loss of situational awareness, or improper task management.
Skills	The applicant demonstrates the ability to:
AA.VI.A.S1	Coordinate with crew, if applicable, and complete the appropriate checklist(s) prior to takeoff in a timely manner.
AA.VI.A.S2	Properly set the applicable avionics and flight instruments prior to initiating the takeoff.
AA.VI.A.S3	Make radio calls as appropriate.
AA.VI.A.S4	Verify assigned/correct runway (ASEL, AMEL) or takeoff path (ASES, AMES).
AA.VI.A.S5	Position the flight controls for the existing wind.
AA.VI.A.S6	Clear the area; taxi into takeoff position and align the airplane on the runway centerline (ASEL, AMEL) or takeoff path (ASES, AMES).
AA.VI.A.S7	Perform an instrument takeoff with instrument meteorological conditions (IMC) simulated at or before reaching an altitude of 100 feet AGL. If accomplished in a full flight simulator, visibility should be no greater than 1/4 mile, or as specified by applicable operations specifications, whichever is lower.
AA.VI.A.S8	Maintain centerline (ASEL, AMEL) and proper flight control inputs during the takeoff roll.
AA.VI.A.S9	Confirm takeoff power and proper engine and flight instrument indications prior to rotation making callouts, as appropriate, for the airplane or per the operator's procedures.
AA.VI.A.S10	Rotate and lift off at the recommended airspeed, establish the desired pitch attitude, and accelerate to the desired airspeed/ V-speed.
AA.VI.A.S11	Transition smoothly from visual meteorological conditions (VMC) to actual or simulated instrument meteorological conditions (IMC).
AA.VI.A.S12	Maintain desired heading ±5° and desired airspeeds ±5 knots.

VI. Instrument Procedures

Task	A. *Instrument Takeoff*
AA.VI.A.S13	Comply with ATC clearances and instructions issued by ATC or the evaluator, as appropriate.
AA.VI.A.S14	Complete appropriate after-takeoff checklist(s) in a timely manner.

VI. Instrument Procedures

Task	B. *Departure Procedures*
References	14 CFR parts 61 and 91; AC 90-100; FAA-H-8083-2, FAA-H-8083-15, FAA-H-8083-16; POH/AFM; AIM; TPP
Objective	To determine that the applicant exhibits satisfactory knowledge, risk management, and skills associated with instrument departure procedures (DPs). ***Note:*** *See Appendix 7: Aircraft, Equipment, and Operational Requirements & Limitations for information related to this Task.*
Knowledge	The applicant demonstrates understanding of:
AA.VI.B.K1	Takeoff minimums; (Obstacle) Departure Procedure (ODP), including Visual Climb over the Airport (VCOA) and Diverse Vector Area (Radar Vectors); Standard Instrument Departure (SID), including RNAV departure; required climb gradients; U.S. Terminal Procedures Publications; and En Route Charts.
AA.VI.B.K2	Use of a Flight Management System (FMS) or Global Positioning System (GPS) to follow a DP.
AA.VI.B.K3	Pilot/controller responsibilities, communication procedures, and ATC services available to pilots.
AA.VI.B.K4	Two-way radio communication failure procedures after takeoff.
AA.VI.B.K5	Ground-based and satellite-based navigation (orientation, course determination, equipment, tests and regulations, interference, appropriate use of navigation data, signal integrity).
Risk Management	The applicant demonstrates the ability to identify, assess, and mitigate risks, encompassing:
AA.VI.B.R1	Failure to communicate with ATC or follow published procedures and required climb gradients.
AA.VI.B.R2	Limitations of air traffic avoidance equipment and use of see and avoid techniques.
AA.VI.B.R3	Improper automation management.
Skills	The applicant demonstrates the ability to:
AA.VI.B.S1	Select the appropriate instrument departure procedure. Then select, identify (as necessary), and use the appropriate communication and navigation facilities associated with the procedure.
AA.VI.B.S2	Program the FMS prior to departure and set avionics to include flight director and autopilot controls, as appropriate, for the departure, if applicable.
AA.VI.B.S3	Coordinate with crew, if applicable, and complete the appropriate checklist(s) in a timely manner.
AA.VI.B.S4	Use current and appropriate navigation publications or databases for the proposed flight.
AA.VI.B.S5	Establish two-way communications with the proper controlling agency, use proper phraseology, comply, in a timely manner, with all ATC instructions and airspace restrictions, and exhibit adequate knowledge of communication failure procedures.
AA.VI.B.S6	Intercept all courses, radials, and bearings appropriate to the procedure, route, clearance, or as directed by the evaluator in a timely manner.
AA.VI.B.S7	Comply with all applicable charted procedures.
AA.VI.B.S8	Maintain the appropriate airspeed ±10 knots, headings ±10°, and altitude ±100 feet, and accurately track a course, radial, or bearing.
AA.VI.B.S9	Conduct the departure phase to a point where, in the opinion of the evaluator, the transition to the en route environment is complete.

VI. Instrument Procedures

Task	C. Arrival Procedures
References	14 CFR parts 61 and 91; AC 90-100; FAA-H-8083-2, FAA-H-8083-15, FAA-H-8083-16; Enroute Low and High Altitude Charts; STARs/FMSPs; TPP; POH/AFM; AIM
Objective	To determine the applicant exhibits satisfactory knowledge, risk management, and skills associated with IFR arrival procedures. **Note:** See Appendix 7: Aircraft, Equipment, and Operational Requirements & Limitations for information related to this Task.
Knowledge	The applicant demonstrates understanding of:
AA.VI.C.K1	Standard Terminal Arrival (STAR) charts, U.S. Terminal Procedures Publications, and IFR Enroute High and Low Altitude Charts.
AA.VI.C.K2	Use of a Flight Management System (FMS) or GPS to follow a STAR.
AA.VI.C.K3	Pilot/controller responsibilities, communication procedures, and ATC services available to pilots.
AA.VI.C.K4	Two-way radio communication failure procedures during an arrival.
AA.VI.C.K5	Ground-based and satellite-based navigation (orientation, course determination, equipment, tests and regulations, interference, appropriate use of navigation data, signal integrity).
Risk Management	The applicant demonstrates the ability to identify, assess, and mitigate risks, encompassing:
AA.VI.C.R1	Failure to communicate with ATC or follow published procedures.
AA.VI.C.R2	Failure to recognize limitations of traffic avoidance equipment.
AA.VI.C.R3	Failure to use see and avoid techniques when possible.
AA.VI.C.R4	Improper automation management.
AA.VI.C.R5	ATC instructions that modify an arrival or discontinue/resume the aircraft's lateral or vertical navigation on an arrival.
Skills	The applicant demonstrates the ability to:
AA.VI.C.S1	In actual or simulated instrument conditions, select, identify (as necessary) and use the appropriate communication and navigation facilities associated with the arrival.
AA.VI.C.S2	Set FMS and avionics to include flight director and autopilot controls for the arrival, if applicable.
AA.VI.C.S3	Coordinate with crew, if applicable, and complete the appropriate checklist(s) in a timely manner.
AA.VI.C.S4	Use current and appropriate navigation publications or databases for the proposed flight.
AA.VI.C.S5	Establish two-way communications with the proper controlling agency, use proper phraseology and comply, in a timely manner, with all ATC instructions and airspace restrictions as well as exhibit adequate knowledge of communication failure procedures.
AA.VI.C.S6	Intercept all courses, radials, and bearings appropriate to the procedure, route, clearance, or as directed by the evaluator in a timely manner.
AA.VI.C.S7	Comply with all applicable charted procedures.
AA.VI.C.S8	Adhere to airspeed restrictions required by regulation, procedure, aircraft limitation, ATC, or the evaluator.
AA.VI.C.S9	Establish rates of descent consistent with the route segment, airplane operating characteristics and safety.
AA.VI.C.S10	Maintain the appropriate airspeed/V-speed ±10 knots, but not less than V_{Ref} if applicable, heading ±10°, altitude ±100 feet, and accurately track radials, courses, and bearings.

VI. Instrument Procedures

Task	D. Nonprecision Approaches
References	14 CFR parts 61 and 91; AC 120-108; FAA-H-8083-15, FAA-H-8083-16; TPP, AIM; Chart Supplements
Objective	To determine that the applicant exhibits satisfactory knowledge, risk management, and skills associated with performing nonprecision approach procedures. **Note:** See Appendix 7: Aircraft, Equipment, and Operational Requirements & Limitations for information related to this Task.
Knowledge	The applicant demonstrates understanding of:
AA.VI.D.K1	Procedures and limitations associated with a nonprecision approach, including the differences between Localizer Performance (LP) and Lateral Navigation (LNAV) approach guidance.
AA.VI.D.K2	Navigation system displays and annunciations, modes of operation, and RNP lateral accuracy values associated with an RNAV (GPS) approach.
AA.VI.D.K3	Ground-based and satellite-based navigation (orientation, course determination, equipment, tests and regulations, interference, appropriate use of navigation data, signal integrity).
AA.VI.D.K4	A stabilized approach, to include energy management concepts.
Risk Management	The applicant demonstrates the ability to identify, assess, and mitigate risks, encompassing:
AA.VI.D.R1	Failure to follow the correct approach procedure (e.g., descending too early, etc.).
AA.VI.D.R2	Selecting an incorrect navigation frequency.
AA.VI.D.R3	Failure to manage automated navigation and autoflight systems.
AA.VI.D.R4	Failure to ensure proper airplane configuration during an approach and missed approach.
AA.VI.D.R5	An unstable approach, including excessive descent rates.
AA.VI.D.R6	Deteriorating weather conditions on approach.
AA.VI.D.R7	Operating below the minimum descent altitude (MDA) or continuing a descent below decision altitude (DA) without proper visual references.
Skills	The applicant demonstrates the ability to:
AA.VI.D.S1	Accomplish the nonprecision instrument approaches selected by the evaluator.
AA.VI.D.S2	Establish two-way communications with ATC appropriate for the phase of flight or approach segment, and use proper communication phraseology.
AA.VI.D.S3	Select, tune, identify, and confirm the operational status of navigation equipment to be used for the approach.
AA.VI.D.S4	Comply with all clearances issued by ATC or the evaluator.
AA.VI.D.S5	Recognize if any flight instrumentation is inaccurate or inoperative, and take appropriate action.
AA.VI.D.S6	Advise ATC or the evaluator if unable to comply with a clearance.
AA.VI.D.S7	Coordinate with crew, if applicable, and complete the appropriate checklist(s) in a timely manner.
AA.VI.D.S8	Establish the appropriate airplane configuration and airspeed considering meteorological and operating conditions.
AA.VI.D.S9	Maintain altitude ±100 feet, selected heading ±5°, airspeed ±10 knots, and accurately track radials, courses, and bearings, prior to beginning the final approach segment.
AA.VI.D.S10	Adjust the published MDA and visibility criteria for the aircraft approach category, as appropriate, for factors that include NOTAMs, inoperative aircraft or navigation equipment, or inoperative visual aids associated with the landing environment, etc.
AA.VI.D.S11	Establish a stabilized descent to the appropriate altitude.
AA.VI.D.S12	For the final approach segment, maintain no more than ¼ scale CDI deflection, airspeed ±5 knots of selected value, and altitude above MDA +50/-0 feet (to the VDP or MAP).

VI. Instrument Procedures

Task	D. Nonprecision Approaches
AA.VI.D.S13	Execute the missed approach procedure if the required visual references are not distinctly visible and identifiable at the appropriate point or altitude for the approach profile; or execute a normal landing from a straight-in or circling approach.
AA.VI.D.S14	Use a Multi-Function Display (MFD) and other graphical navigation displays, if installed, to monitor position, track wind drift and other parameters to maintain desired flightpath.

VI. Instrument Procedures

Task	E. Precision Approaches
References	14 CFR parts 61 and 91; FAA-H-8083-15, FAA-H-8083-16; TPP; AIM; Chart Supplements
Objective	To determine that the applicant exhibits satisfactory knowledge, risk management, and skills associated with performing precision approach procedures. **Note:** *See Appendix 7: Aircraft, Equipment, and Operational Requirements & Limitations for information related to this Task.*
Knowledge	The applicant demonstrates understanding of:
AA.VI.E.K1	Procedures and limitations associated with a precision approach, including determining required descent rates and adjusting minimums in the case of inoperative equipment.
AA.VI.E.K2	Navigation system displays, annunciations, and modes of operation.
AA.VI.E.K3	Ground-based and satellite-based navigation (orientation, course determination, equipment, tests and regulations, interference, appropriate use of navigation data, signal integrity).
AA.VI.E.K4	A stabilized approach, to include energy management concepts.
Risk Management	The applicant demonstrates the ability to identify, assess, and mitigate risks, encompassing:
AA.VI.E.R1	Failure to follow the correct approach procedure (e.g. descending below the glideslope, etc.).
AA.VI.E.R2	Selecting an incorrect navigation frequency.
AA.VI.E.R3	Failure to manage automated navigation and autoflight systems.
AA.VI.E.R4	Failure to ensure proper airplane configuration during an approach and missed approach.
AA.VI.E.R5	An unstable approach, including excessive descent rates.
AA.VI.E.R6	Deteriorating weather conditions on approach.
AA.VI.E.R7	Continuing to descend below the Decision Altitude (DA)/Decision Height (DH) when the required visual references are not visible.
Skills	The applicant demonstrates the ability to:
AA.VI.E.S1	Accomplish the precision instrument approaches selected by the evaluator.
AA.VI.E.S2	Establish two-way communications with ATC appropriate for the phase of flight or approach segment, and use proper communication phraseology.
AA.VI.E.S3	Select, tune, identify, and confirm the operational status of navigation equipment to be used for the approach.
AA.VI.E.S4	Comply in a timely manner with all clearances, instructions, and procedures.
AA.VI.E.S5	Recognize if any flight instrumentation is inaccurate or inoperative, and take appropriate action.
AA.VI.E.S6	Advise ATC or the evaluator if unable to comply with a clearance.
AA.VI.E.S7	Coordinate with crew, if applicable, and complete the appropriate checklist(s) in a timely manner.
AA.VI.E.S8	Establish the appropriate airplane configuration and airspeed considering meteorological and operating conditions.
AA.VI.E.S9	Maintain altitude ±100 feet, heading ±5°, airspeed ±10 knots, and accurately track radials, courses, and bearings, prior to beginning the final approach segment.
AA.VI.E.S10	Adjust the published DA/DH and visibility criteria for the aircraft approach category, as appropriate, to account for NOTAMS, inoperative airplane or navigation equipment, or inoperative visual aids associated with the landing environment.
AA.VI.E.S11	Establish a predetermined rate of descent at the point where vertical guidance begins, which approximates that required for the aircraft to follow the vertical guidance.
AA.VI.E.S12	Maintain a stabilized final approach from the Final Approach Fix (FAF) to DA/DH allowing no more than ¼-scale deflection of either the vertical or lateral guidance indications and maintain the desired airspeed ±5 knots.

VI. Instrument Procedures

Task	E. Precision Approaches
AA.VI.E.S13	Upon reaching the DA/DH, immediately initiate the missed approach procedures if the required visual references for the runway are not distinctly visible and identifiable (or if in a seaplane); or transition to a normal landing approach only when the aircraft is in a position from which a descent to a landing on the runway can be made at a normal rate of descent using normal maneuvering.
AA.VI.E.S14	Use an MFD and other graphical navigation displays, if installed, to monitor position, track wind drift and other parameters to maintain desired flightpath.

VI. Instrument Procedures

Task	F. Landing from a Precision Approach
References	14 CFR parts 61 and 91; FAA-H-8083-15, FAA-H-8083-16; SAFO 19001; AIM
Objective	To determine that the applicant exhibits satisfactory knowledge, risk management, and skills associated with performing the procedures for a landing from a precision approach. *Note: See Appendix 7: Aircraft, Equipment, and Operational Requirements & Limitations for information related to this Task.*
Knowledge	The applicant demonstrates understanding of:
AA.VI.F.K1	Elements related to the pilot's responsibilities, and the environmental, operational, and meteorological factors that affect landing from a precision approach.
AA.VI.F.K2	Approach lighting systems and runway and taxiway signs, markings and lighting.
Risk Management	The applicant demonstrates the ability to identify, assess, and mitigate risks, encompassing:
AA.VI.F.R1	Selection of an approach procedure and runway based on pilot capability, aircraft limitations, available distance, surface conditions, and wind.
AA.VI.F.R2	Wake turbulence.
AA.VI.F.R3	Planning for:
AA.VI.F.R3a	a. Missed approach
AA.VI.F.R3b	b. Land and hold short operations (LAHSO)
AA.VI.F.R4	Collision hazards, to include aircraft, terrain, obstacles, wires, vehicles, vessels, persons, and wildlife.
AA.VI.F.R5	Low altitude maneuvering including stall, spin, or CFIT.
AA.VI.F.R6	Distractions, loss of situational awareness, or improper task management.
AA.VI.F.R7	Attempting to land from an unstable approach.
AA.VI.F.R8	Flying below the glidepath.
AA.VI.F.R9	Transitioning from instrument to visual references for landing.
Skills	The applicant demonstrates the ability to:
AA.VI.F.S1	Maintain the desired airspeed, ±5 knots, and vertical and lateral guidance within ¼-scale deflection of the indicators during the descent from DA/DH to a point where visual maneuvering is used to accomplish a normal landing.
AA.VI.F.S2	Adhere to all ATC or evaluator advisories, such as NOTAMs, windshear, wake turbulence, runway surface, braking conditions, and other operational considerations.
AA.VI.F.S3	Coordinate with crew, if applicable, and complete the appropriate checklist(s) in a timely manner.
AA.VI.F.S4	Touch down at the aiming point markings, -250/+500 feet, or where there are no runway aiming point markings, 750 to 1,500 feet, from the approach threshold of the runway.
AA.VI.F.S5	Maintain positive airplane control throughout the landing using drag and braking devices, as appropriate, to come to a stop.
AA.VI.F.S6	Demonstrate SRM or CRM, as appropriate.
AA.VI.F.S7	Utilize runway incursion avoidance procedures.

VI. Instrument Procedures

Task	G. Circling Approach
References	14 CFR parts 61, 91, and 97; FAA-H-8083-15, FAA-H-8083-16; AIM; TPP; Chart Supplements
Objective	To determine that the applicant exhibits satisfactory knowledge, risk management, and skills associated with performing a circling approach procedure. ***Note:*** *See Appendix 7: Aircraft, Equipment, and Operational Requirements & Limitations for information related to this Task.*
Knowledge	The applicant demonstrates understanding of:
AA.VI.G.K1	Elements related to circling approach procedures and limitations including approach categories and related airspeed restrictions.
Risk Management	The applicant demonstrates the ability to identify, assess, and mitigate risks, encompassing:
AA.VI.G.R1	Failure to follow prescribed circling approach procedures.
AA.VI.G.R2	Executing a circling approach at night or with marginal visibility.
AA.VI.G.R3	Losing visual contact with an identifiable part of the airport.
AA.VI.G.R4	Failure to manage automated navigation and autoflight systems.
AA.VI.G.R5	Failure to maintain an appropriate altitude or airspeed while circling.
AA.VI.G.R6	Low altitude maneuvering including stall, spin, or CFIT.
AA.VI.G.R7	Executing an improper missed approach after the MAP while circling.
Skills	The applicant demonstrates the ability to:
AA.VI.G.S1	Comply with the circling approach procedure considering turbulence, windshear, and the maneuvering capability and approach category of the aircraft.
AA.VI.G.S2	Confirm the direction of traffic and adhere to all restrictions and instructions issued by ATC or the evaluator.
AA.VI.G.S3	Coordinate with crew, if applicable, and complete the appropriate checklist(s) in a timely manner.
AA.VI.G.S4	Establish the approach and landing configuration. Maintain a stabilized approach and a descent rate that ensures arrival at the MDA, or the preselected circling altitude above the MDA, prior to the missed approach point.
AA.VI.G.S5	Maintain airspeed ±5 knots, desired heading/track ±5°, and altitude +100/-0 feet until descending below the MDA or the preselected circling altitude above the MDA.
AA.VI.G.S6	Visually maneuver to a base or downwind leg appropriate for the landing runway and environmental conditions.
AA.VI.G.S7	If a missed approach occurs, turn in the appropriate direction using the correct procedure and appropriately configure the airplane.

VI. Instrument Procedures

Task	H. Landing from a Circling Approach
References	14 CFR parts 61 and 91; FAA-H-8083-15, FAA-H-8083-16; SAFO 19001; AIM
Objective	To determine that the applicant exhibits satisfactory knowledge, risk management, and skills associated with performing the procedures for a landing from a circling approach. *Note: See Appendix 7: Aircraft, Equipment, and Operational Requirements & Limitations for information related to this Task.*
Knowledge	The applicant demonstrates understanding of:
AA.VI.H.K1	Elements related to the pilot's responsibilities, and the environmental, operational, and meteorological factors that affect landing from a circling approach.
AA.VI.H.K2	Approach lighting systems and runway and taxiway signs, markings and lighting.
Risk Management	The applicant demonstrates the ability to identify, assess, and mitigate risks, encompassing:
AA.VI.H.R1	Selection of an approach procedure and runway based on pilot capability, aircraft limitations, available distance, surface conditions, and wind.
AA.VI.H.R2	Wake turbulence.
AA.VI.H.R3	Planning for:
AA.VI.H.R3a	a. Missed approach
AA.VI.H.R3b	b. Land and hold short operations (LAHSO)
AA.VI.H.R4	Collision hazards, to include aircraft, terrain, obstacles, wires, vehicles, vessels, persons, and wildlife.
AA.VI.H.R5	Low altitude maneuvering including stall, spin, or CFIT.
AA.VI.H.R6	Distractions, loss of situational awareness, or improper task management.
AA.VI.H.R7	Attempting to land from an unstable approach.
Skills	The applicant demonstrates the ability to:
AA.VI.H.S1	Keep the airport environment in sight and remain within the circling approach radius applicable to the approach category to a position from which a stabilized descent to landing can be made.
AA.VI.H.S2	Adhere to all ATC or evaluator advisories, such as NOTAMs, windshear, wake turbulence, runway surface, braking conditions, and other operational considerations.
AA.VI.H.S3	Coordinate with crew, if applicable, and complete the appropriate checklist(s) in a timely manner.
AA.VI.H.S4	Aligns the airplane for a normal landing on the selected runway without excessive maneuvering and without exceeding the normal operating limits of the airplane. The angle of bank should not exceed 30°.
AA.VI.H.S5	Make smooth, timely, and correct control application throughout the circling maneuver and maintain appropriate airspeed, ±5 knots. If applicable, maintain altitude +100/−0 feet, and desired heading/track, ±5°.
AA.VI.H.S6	Ensure the airplane is configured for landing.
AA.VI.H.S7	Scan the landing runway and adjoining area for traffic and obstructions. (ASEL, AMEL).
AA.VI.H.S8	Touch down at the aiming point markings - 250/+500 feet, or where there are no runway aiming point markings 750 to 1,500 feet from the approach threshold of the runway.
AA.VI.H.S9	Maintain positive aircraft control throughout the landing using drag and braking devices, as appropriate, to come to a stop.
AA.VI.H.S10	Demonstrate SRM or CRM, as appropriate.
AA.VI.H.S11	Utilize runway incursion avoidance procedures.

VI. Instrument Procedures

Task	I. *Missed Approaches*
References	14 CFR parts 61 and 91; FAA-H-8083-15, FAA-H-8083-16; TPP; AIM
Objective	To determine that the applicant exhibits satisfactory knowledge, risk management, and skills associated with performing a missed approach procedure. ***Note:*** *See Appendix 7: Aircraft, Equipment, and Operational Requirements & Limitations for information related to this Task.*
Knowledge	The applicant demonstrates understanding of:
AA.VI.I.K1	Elements related to missed approach procedures to include reference to standby or backup instruments.
AA.VI.I.K2	Limitations associated with standard instrument approaches, including while using an FMS or autopilot, if equipped.
Risk Management	The applicant demonstrates the ability to identify, assess, and mitigate risks, encompassing:
AA.VI.I.R1	Failure to follow prescribed procedures.
AA.VI.I.R2	Holding, diverting, or electing to fly the approach again.
AA.VI.I.R3	Failure to ensure proper airplane configuration during an approach and missed approach.
AA.VI.I.R4	Factors that might lead to executing a missed approach procedure before the MAP or to a go-around below DA/MDA.
AA.VI.I.R5	Failure to manage automated navigation and autoflight systems.
Skills	The applicant demonstrates the ability to:
AA.VI.I.S1	Promptly initiate the missed approach procedure and report it to ATC.
AA.VI.I.S2	Apply the appropriate power setting for the flight condition and establish a pitch attitude necessary to obtain the desired performance.
AA.VI.I.S3	Retract the wing flaps/drag devices and landing gear, if appropriate, in the correct sequence and at a safe altitude, and establish a positive rate of climb and the appropriate airspeed/V-speed, ±5 knots.
AA.VI.I.S4	Coordinate with crew, if applicable, and complete the appropriate procedures and checklist(s) in a timely manner.
AA.VI.I.S5	Comply with the published or alternate missed approach procedure.
AA.VI.I.S6	Advise ATC or the evaluator if unable to comply with a clearance, restriction, or climb gradient.
AA.VI.I.S7	Maintain the heading, course, or bearing ±5°, and altitude(s) ±100 feet during the missed approach procedure.
AA.VI.I.S8	Use an MFD and other graphical navigation displays, if installed, to monitor position and track to help navigate the missed approach.
AA.VI.I.S9	Demonstrate SRM or CRM, as appropriate.
AA.VI.I.S10	Re-engage autopilot (if installed) at appropriate times during the missed approach procedure.
AA.VI.I.S11	Request ATC clearance to attempt another approach, proceed to the alternate airport, holding fix, or other clearance limit, as appropriate, or as directed by the evaluator.

VI. Instrument Procedures

Task	J. Holding Procedures
References	14 CFR parts 61 and 91; AC 91-74; FAA-H-8083-15, FAA-H-8083-16; POH/AFM; AIM; TPP
Objective	To determine that the applicant exhibits satisfactory knowledge, risk management, and skills associated with holding procedures. ***Note:*** *See Appendix 7: Aircraft, Equipment, and Operational Requirements & Limitations for information related to this Task.*
Knowledge	The applicant demonstrates understanding of:
AA.VI.J.K1	Elements related to holding procedures, including reporting criteria, appropriate speeds, and recommended entry procedures for standard, nonstandard, published, and non-published holding patterns.
AA.VI.J.K2	Determining holding endurance based upon factors to include an expect further clearance (EFC) time, fuel on board, fuel flow while holding, fuel required to destination and alternate, etc., as appropriate.
AA.VI.J.K3	When to declare minimum fuel or a fuel-related emergency.
AA.VI.J.K4	Use of automation for holding to include autopilot and flight management systems, if equipped.
Risk Management	The applicant demonstrates the ability to identify, assess, and mitigate risks, encompassing:
AA.VI.J.R1	Recalculating fuel reserves if assigned an unanticipated EFC time.
AA.VI.J.R2	Scenarios and circumstances that could result in minimum fuel or the need to declare an emergency.
AA.VI.J.R3	Scenarios that could lead to holding, including deteriorating weather at the planned destination.
AA.VI.J.R4	Improper holding entry and improper wind correction while holding.
AA.VI.J.R5	Holding while in icing conditions.
AA.VI.J.R6	Improper automation management.
Skills	The applicant demonstrates the ability to:
AA.VI.J.S1	Correctly identifies instrument navigation aids associated with the assigned hold.
AA.VI.J.S2	Uses an entry procedure appropriate for a standard, nonstandard, published, or non-published holding pattern.
AA.VI.J.S3	Changes to the appropriate holding airspeed for the airplane and holding altitude to cross the holding fix at or below maximum holding airspeed.
AA.VI.J.S4	Comply with the holding pattern leg length and other restrictions, if applicable, associated with the holding pattern.
AA.VI.J.S5	Comply with ATC reporting requirements.
AA.VI.J.S6	Use proper wind correction procedures to maintain the desired pattern and to arrive over the fix as close as possible to a specified time.
AA.VI.J.S7	Maintain the airspeed ±10 knots, altitude ±100 feet, headings ±10°, and accurately track a selected course, radial, or bearing.
AA.VI.J.S8	If available, uses automation to include autopilot, flight director controls, and navigation displays associated with the assigned hold.
AA.VI.J.S9	Update fuel reserve calculations based on EFC times.

VII. Emergency Operations

Task	A. Emergency Procedures
References	14 CFR part 91; AC 91-74; FAA-H-8083-2, FAA-H-8083-3, FAA-H-8083-23, FAA-H-8083-25; POH/AFM; AIM; FSB Report (type specific)
Objective	To determine that the applicant exhibits satisfactory knowledge, risk management, and skills associated with emergency procedures.
Knowledge	The applicant demonstrates understanding of:
AA.VII.A.K1	Declaring an emergency and selection of a suitable airport or landing location.
AA.VII.A.K2	Situations that would require an emergency descent (e.g., depressurization, smoke, or engine fire).
AA.VII.A.K3	Causes of inflight fire or smoke.
AA.VII.A.K4	Airplane decompression.
AA.VII.A.K5	When an emergency evacuation may be necessary.
AA.VII.A.K6	Actions required if icing conditions exceed the capabilities of the airplane.
Risk Management	The applicant demonstrates the ability to identify, assess, and mitigate risks, encompassing:
AA.VII.A.R1	Failure to follow proper procedures or checklists in an emergency.
AA.VII.A.R2	Multiple failures or system abnormalities.
AA.VII.A.R3	Failure to consider altitude, wind, terrain, and obstructions in an emergency.
AA.VII.A.R4	Distractions, loss of situational awareness, or improper task management.
Skills	For the airplane provided for the practical test, the applicant demonstrates the ability to:
AA.VII.A.S1	Explain or describe an emergency procedure for a situation(s) presented by the evaluator.
AA.VII.A.S2	Use proper procedures for an emergency situation(s) presented by the evaluator, such as:
AA.VII.A.S2a	a. Emergency descent
AA.VII.A.S2b	b. Inflight fire and smoke
AA.VII.A.S2c	c. Decompression
AA.VII.A.S2d	d. Emergency evacuation
AA.VII.A.S2e	e. Airframe icing
AA.VII.A.S2f	f. Others as specified in the AFM/POH
AA.VII.A.S3	Fly by reference to standby flight instruments, backup instrumentation, or partial panel, if applicable and appropriate to the situation.
AA.VII.A.S4	Coordinate with crew, if applicable, and complete the appropriate checklist(s) in a timely manner.
AA.VII.A.S5	Communicate with ATC and the evaluator, as appropriate for the situation.

VII. Emergency Operations

Task	B. Powerplant Failure during Takeoff
References	FAA-H-8083-2, FAA-H-8083-3; POH/AFM; FSB Report (type specific)
Objective	To determine that the applicant exhibits satisfactory knowledge, risk management, and skills associated with a powerplant failure during takeoff. *Note: See Appendix 6: Safety of Flight and Appendix 7: Aircraft, Equipment, and Operational Requirements & Limitations for information related to this Task.*
Knowledge	The applicant demonstrates understanding of:
AA.VII.B.K1	The procedures used during a powerplant failure on takeoff, the appropriate reference airspeeds, and the specific pilot actions required.
AA.VII.B.K2	Operational considerations to include: airplane performance (e.g., sideslip, bank angle, rudder input), takeoff warning systems, runway length, surface conditions, density altitude, wake turbulence, environmental conditions, obstructions, and other related factors that could adversely affect safety.
Risk Management	The applicant demonstrates the ability to identify, assess, and mitigate risks, encompassing:
AA.VII.B.R1	Failure to plan for a powerplant failure during takeoff considering operational factors such as takeoff warning inhibit systems, other airplane characteristics, runway/takeoff path length, surface conditions, environmental conditions, obstructions, and LAHSO operations.
AA.VII.B.R2	Failure to brief the plan for a powerplant failure during takeoff, in a crew environment.
AA.VII.B.R3	Failure to follow proper procedures or checklists in an emergency.
AA.VII.B.R4	Failure to correctly identify the inoperative engine (AMEL, AMES).
AA.VII.B.R5	Inability to climb or maintain altitude with an inoperative powerplant (AMEL, AMES).
AA.VII.B.R6	Failure to consider altitude, wind, terrain, and obstructions in an emergency.
AA.VII.B.R7	Low altitude maneuvering including stall, spin, or CFIT.
AA.VII.B.R8	Distractions, loss of situational awareness, or improper task management.
Skills	The applicant demonstrates the ability to:
AA.VII.B.S1	Following the powerplant failure, maintain positive airplane control and adjust the powerplant controls as recommended by the manufacturer for the existing conditions.
AA.VII.B.S2	Establish a power-off descent approximately straight-ahead, if the powerplant failure occurs after becoming airborne and before reaching an altitude where a safe turn can be made (ASEL, ASES) or the performance capabilities and operating limitations of the airplane will not allow the climb to continue (AMEL, AMES).
AA.VII.B.S3	Continue the takeoff if the (simulated) powerplant failure occurs at a point where the airplane can continue to a specified airspeed and altitude at the end of the runway commensurate with the airplane's performance capabilities and operating limitations(AMEL, AMES).
AA.VII.B.S4	After establishing a climb, maintain the desired airspeed, ±5 knots. Use flight controls in the proper combination as recommended by the manufacturer, or as required, to maintain best performance and trim as required (AMEL, AMES).
AA.VII.B.S5	Maintain the appropriate heading, ±5°, when powerplant failure occurs (AMEL, AMES).
AA.VII.B.S6	Coordinate with crew, if applicable, and complete the appropriate checklist(s) following the powerplant failure.
AA.VII.B.S7	Communicate with ATC and the evaluator, as appropriate for the situation.

VII. Emergency Operations

Task	C. Powerplant Failure (Simulated) (ASEL, ASES)
References	FAA-H-8083-2, FAA-H-8083-3; POH/AFM
Objective	To determine that the applicant exhibits satisfactory knowledge, risk management, and skills associated with a powerplant failure and associated emergency approach and landing procedures. **Note:** *See Appendix 6: Safety of Flight and Appendix 7: Aircraft, Equipment, and Operational Requirements & Limitations for information related to this Task.*
Knowledge	The applicant demonstrates understanding of:
AA.VII.C.K1	Immediate action items and emergency procedures for a forced landing.
AA.VII.C.K2	Airspeed, to include:
AA.VII.C.K2a	a. Importance of best glide speed and its relationship to distance
AA.VII.C.K2b	b. Difference between best glide speed and minimum sink speed
AA.VIII.C.K2c	c. Effects of wind on glide distance
AA.VII.C.K3	Effects of atmospheric conditions on emergency approach and landing.
AA.VII.C.K4	A stabilized approach, to include energy management concepts.
AA.VII.C.K5	Emergency Locator Transmitter (ELTs) and other emergency locating devices.
AA.VII.C.K6	ATC services to aircraft in distress.
Risk Management	The applicant demonstrates the ability to identify, assess, and mitigate risks, encompassing:
AA.VII.C.R1	Failure to consider altitude, wind, terrain, obstructions, gliding distance, and available landing distance.
AA.VII.C.R2	Failure to plan and follow a flightpath to the selected landing area.
AA.VII.C.R3	Collision hazards, to include aircraft, terrain, obstacles, wires, vehicles, vessels, persons, and wildlife.
AA.VII.C.R4	Improper airplane configuration.
AA.VII.C.R5	Low altitude maneuvering including stall, spin, or CFIT.
AA.VII.C.R6	Distractions, loss of situational awareness, or improper task management.
AA.VII.C.R7	A powerplant failure in IMC conditions.
Skills	The applicant demonstrates the ability to:
AA.VII.C.S1	Recognize the powerplant failure.
AA.VII.C.S2	Determine the cause for the simulated powerplant failure (if altitude permits) and if a restart is a viable option.
AA.VII.C.S3	Maintain positive control throughout the maneuver.
AA.VII.C.S4	Establish and maintain the recommended best glide airspeed, ±5 knots.
AA.VII.C.S5	Configure the airplane in accordance with the POH/AFM and existing conditions.
AA.VII.C.S6	Select a suitable landing area considering altitude, wind, terrain, obstructions, and available glide distance.
AA.VII.C.S7	Establish a proper flight path to the selected landing area.
AA.VII.C.S8	Complete emergency checklist items appropriate to the airplane in a timely manner and as recommended by the manufacturer or operator.
AA.VII.C.S9	Communicate with ATC and the evaluator, as appropriate for the situation.

VII. Emergency Operations

Task	D. Inflight Powerplant Failure and Restart (AMEL, AMES)
References	FAA-H-8083-2, FAA-H-8083-3; POH/AFM
Objective	To determine that the applicant exhibits satisfactory knowledge, risk management, and skills associated with an inflight powerplant failure in a multiengine airplane and restart procedures. **Note:** See Appendix 6: Safety of Flight and Appendix 7: Aircraft, Equipment, and Operational Requirements & Limitations for information related to this Task.
Knowledge	The applicant demonstrates understanding of:
AA.VII.D.K1	Flight characteristics and controllability associated with maneuvering the airplane with powerplant(s) inoperative to include the importance of drag reduction.
AA.VII.D.K2	Powerplant restart procedures and conditions where a restart attempt is appropriate.
Risk Management	The applicant demonstrates the ability to identify, assess, and mitigate risks, encompassing:
AA.VII.D.R1	Failure to plan for a powerplant failure during flight.
AA.VII.D.R2	Failure to follow checklist procedures for a powerplant failure or a powerplant restart.
AA.VII.D.R3	Incorrect diagnosis of the cause of the powerplant failure.
AA.VII.D.R4	Collision hazards, to include aircraft, terrain, obstacles, wires, vehicles, vessels, persons, and wildlife.
AA.VII.D.R5	Improper airplane configuration.
AA.VII.D.R6	Factors and situations that could lead to an inadvertent stall, spin, and loss of control with an inflight powerplant failure.
AA.VII.D.R7	Distractions, loss of situational awareness, or improper task management.
Skills	The applicant demonstrates the ability to:
AA.VII.D.S1	Recognize and correctly identify powerplant failure(s), complete memory items (if applicable), and maintain positive airplane control.
AA.VII.D.S2	Coordinate with crew, as appropriate, and complete the appropriate emergency procedures and checklist(s) for propeller feathering or powerplant shutdown.
AA.VII.D.S3	Use flight controls in the proper combination as recommended by the manufacturer, or as required, to maintain best performance, and trim as required.
AA.VII.D.S4	Determine the cause for the powerplant(s) failure and if a restart is a viable option.
AA.VII.D.S5	Maintain the operating powerplant(s) within acceptable operating limits.
AA.VII.D.S6	Maintain the airspeed ±10 knots, the specified heading ±10°, and altitude ±100 feet as specified by the evaluator and within the airplane's capability.
AA.VII.D.S7	Consider a powerplant restart and, if appropriate, demonstrate the powerplant restart procedures in accordance with the manufacturer or operator specified procedures and checklists.
AA.VII.D.S8	Select the nearest suitable airport or landing area.
AA.VII.D.S9	Communicate with ATC and the evaluator, as appropriate for the situation.

VII. Emergency Operations

Task	E. *Approach and Landing with a Powerplant Failure (Simulated) (AMEL, AMES)*
References	FAA-H-8083-2, FAA-H-8083-3; SAFO 19001; POH/AFM
Objective	To determine that the applicant exhibits satisfactory knowledge, risk management, and skills associated with an approach and landing with a powerplant failure in a multiengine airplane. **Note:** See Appendix 6: Safety of Flight and Appendix 7: Aircraft, Equipment, and Operational Requirements & Limitations for information related to this Task.
Knowledge	The applicant demonstrates understanding of:
AA.VII.E.K1	Flight characteristics and controllability associated with maneuvering to a landing with inoperative powerplant(s).
AA.VII.E.K2	Go-around/rejected landing procedures with a powerplant failure.
AA.VII.E.K3	How to determine a suitable airport.
Risk Management	The applicant demonstrates the ability to identify, assess, and mitigate risks, encompassing:
AA.VII.E.R1	Failure to plan for a powerplant failure inflight or during an approach.
AA.VII.E.R2	Collision hazards, to include aircraft, terrain, obstacles, wires, vehicles, vessels, persons, and wildlife.
AA.VII.E.R3	Improper airplane configuration.
AA.VII.E.R4	Low altitude maneuvering including stall, spin, or CFIT.
AA.VII.E.R5	Distractions, loss of situational awareness, or improper task management.
AA.VII.E.R6	Performing a go-around/rejected landing with a powerplant failure.
Skills	The applicant demonstrates the ability to:
AA.VII.E.S1	Recognize and correctly identify powerplant failure(s), complete memory items (if applicable), and maintain positive airplane control.
AA.VII.E.S2	Coordinate with crew, if applicable, and complete the appropriate emergency procedures and checklist(s) for simulated propeller feathering or simulated powerplant shutdown.
AA.VII.E.S3	Use flight controls in the proper combination as recommended by the manufacturer, or as required, to maintain best performance, and trim as required.
AA.VII.E.S4	Maintain the operating powerplant(s) within acceptable operating limits.
AA.VII.E.S5	Communicate with ATC and the evaluator, as appropriate for the situation.
AA.VII.E.S6	Prior to beginning the final approach segment, maintain the desired altitude ±100 feet, the desired airspeed ±10 knots, the desired heading ±5°, and accurately track courses, radials, and bearings.
AA.VII.E.S7	Establish the recommended approach and landing configuration and airspeed, ±5 knots, and adjust pitch attitude and power as required to maintain a stabilized approach.
AA.VII.E.S8	Maintain directional control and appropriate crosswind correction throughout the approach and landing.
AA.VII.E.S9	Make smooth, timely, and correct control application before, during, and after touchdown.
AA.VII.E.S10	Touch down at the appropriate speed and pitch attitude at the runway aiming point markings -250/+500 feet, or where there are no runway markings 750 to 1,500 feet from the approach threshold of the runway. (AMEL)
AA.VII.E.S11	During round out and touchdown contact the water at the proper pitch attitude within 200 feet beyond a specified point. In addition, for AMES, the touchdown will be within the first one-third of the water landing area.
AA.VII.E.S12	Maintain positive aircraft control throughout the landing using drag and braking devices, as appropriate, to come to a stop.
AA.VII.E.S13	Coordinate with crew, if applicable, and complete after landing checklists.

VII. Emergency Operations

Task	F. Precision Approach (Manually Flown) with a Powerplant Failure (Simulated) (AMEL, AMES)
References	FAA-H-8083-2, FAA-H-8083-3, FAA-H-8083-15, FAA-H-8083-16; POH/AFM; TPP
Objective	To determine that the applicant exhibits satisfactory knowledge, risk management, and skills associated with a precision approach (manually flown) with a powerplant failure in a multiengine airplane. *Note:* See Appendix 6: Safety of Flight and Appendix 7: Aircraft, Equipment, and Operational Requirements & Limitations for information related to this Task.
Knowledge	The applicant demonstrates understanding of:
AA.VII.F.K1	Flight characteristics and controllability associated with maneuvering to a landing with inoperative powerplant(s).
AA.VII.F.K2	Missed approach considerations with a powerplant failure.
AA.VII.F.K3	How to determine a suitable airport.
Risk Management	The applicant demonstrates the ability to identify, assess, and mitigate risks, encompassing:
AA.VII.F.R1	Failure to plan for a powerplant failure inflight or during an approach.
AA.VII.F.R2	Collision hazards, to include aircraft, terrain, obstacles, wires, vehicles, vessels, persons, and wildlife.
AA.VII.F.R3	Improper airplane configuration.
AA.VII.F.R4	Low altitude maneuvering including stall, spin, or CFIT.
AA.VII.F.R5	Distractions, loss of situational awareness, or improper task management.
AA.VII.F.R6	Landing with a powerplant failure.
AA.VII.F.R7	Missed approach with a powerplant failure.
AA.VII.F.R8	Maneuvering in IMC with a powerplant failure.
Skills	The applicant demonstrates the ability to:
AA.VII.F.S1	Recognize and correctly identify powerplant failure(s), complete memory items (if applicable), and maintain positive airplane control.
AA.VII.F.S2	Coordinate with crew, if applicable, and complete the appropriate emergency procedures and checklist(s) for simulated propeller feathering or simulated powerplant shutdown.
AA.VII.F.S3	Use flight controls in the proper combination as recommended by the manufacturer, or as required, to maintain best performance, and trim as required.
AA.VII.F.S4	Maintain the operating powerplant(s) within acceptable operating limits.
AA.VII.F.S5	Make radio calls, as appropriate.
AA.VII.F.S6	Proceed toward the nearest suitable airport.
AA.VII.F.S7	Coordinate with crew, if applicable, and complete the approach and landing checklists.
AA.VII.F.S8	Establish the appropriate airplane configuration and airspeed considering meteorological and operating conditions.
AA.VII.F.S9	Prior to beginning the final approach segment, maintain the desired altitude ±100 feet, the desired airspeed ±10 knots, the desired heading ±5°, and accurately track courses, radials, and bearings.
AA.VII.F.S10	Apply adjustments to the published DA/DH and visibility criteria for the aircraft approach category, as appropriate, for factors that include NOTAMs, Inoperative aircraft or navigation equipment, inoperative visual aids associated with the landing environment, etc.
AA.VII.F.S11	Establish a predetermined rate of descent at the point where vertical guidance begins, which approximates that required for the aircraft to follow the vertical guidance.
AA.VII.F.S12	Fly and maintain a stabilized approach, adjusting pitch and power as required, allowing no more than ¼-scale deflection of either the vertical or lateral guidance indications.

VII. Emergency Operations

Task	F. Precision Approach (Manually Flown) with a Powerplant Failure (Simulated) (AMEL, AMES)
AA.VII.F.S13	Maintain a stabilized final approach from the FAF to the DA/DH allowing no more than ¼-scale deflection of either the vertical or lateral guidance indications and maintain the desired airspeed ±5 knots.
AA.VII.F.S14	Maintain directional control and appropriate crosswind correction throughout the approach and landing or missed approach.
AA.VII.F.S15	Upon reaching the DA/DH, immediately initiate the missed approach procedure if the required visual references for the runway are not distinctly visible and identifiable (or if in a seaplane); or transition to a normal landing approach only when the aircraft is in a position from which a descent to a landing on the runway can be made at a normal rate of descent using normal maneuvering.
AA.VII.F.S16	Make smooth, timely, and correct control application before, during, and after touchdown or during the missed approach.

VII. Emergency Operations

Task	G. Landing from a No Flap or a Nonstandard Flap Approach
References	FAA-H-8083-2, FAA-H-8083-3; POH/AFM; SAFO 19001; FSB Report (type specific)
Objective	To determine that the applicant exhibits satisfactory knowledge, risk management, and skills associated with a no flap or a nonstandard flap approach and landing. ***Note***: *See Appendix 7: Aircraft, Equipment, and Operational Requirements & Limitations for information related to this Task.*
Knowledge	The applicant demonstrates understanding of:
AA.VII.G.K1	Airplane flight characteristics when flaps, leading edge devices, and other similar devices malfunction or become inoperative.
AA.VII.G.K2	Other airplane system limitations when landing at a high speed.
AA.VII.G.K3	How to determine required landing distance and a suitable runway for landing.
Risk Management	The applicant demonstrates the ability to identify, assess, and mitigate risks, encompassing:
AA.VII.G.R1	Hazards associated with a no flap or nonstandard flap approach and landing to include an asymmetrical flap situation.
AA.VII.G.R2	Selection of a runway based on pilot capability, aircraft limitations, available distance, surface conditions, and wind.
AA.VII.G.R3	Wake turbulence.
AA.VII.G.R4	Go-around/rejected landing.
AA.VII.G.R5	Collision hazards, to include aircraft, terrain, obstacles, wires, vehicles, vessels, persons, and wildlife.
AA.VII.G.R6	Low altitude maneuvering including stall, spin, or CFIT.
AA.VII.G.R7	Distractions, loss of situational awareness, or improper task management.
Skills	The applicant demonstrates the ability to:
AA.VII.G.S1	Identify the malfunction.
AA.VII.G.S2	Coordinate with crew, if applicable, and complete applicable checklist(s) for the malfunction, approach, and landing.
AA.VII.G.S3	Communicate with ATC as needed and select an airport/runway with sufficient length for landing.
AA.VII.G.S4	Calculate the correct airspeeds/V-speeds for approach and landing.
AA.VII.G.S5	Establish the recommended approach and landing configuration and airspeed, and adjust pitch attitude and power as required to maintain a stabilized approach.
AA.VII.G.S6	Select a suitable touchdown point considering wind, landing surface, and obstructions.
AA.VII.G.S7	Make smooth, timely, and correct control application before, during, and after touchdown.
AA.VII.G.S8	Touch down at an acceptable point on the runway. Touch down at the appropriate speed and pitch attitude at the runway aiming point markings -250/+500 feet, or where there are no runway markings 750 to 1,500 feet from the approach threshold of the runway. (ASEL, AMEL)
AA.VII.G.S9	Touch down at an acceptable point on the landing surface. During round out and touchdown contact the water at the proper pitch attitude within 200 feet beyond a specified point (ASES, AMES). In addition, for AMES, the touchdown will be within the first one-third of the water landing area.
AA.VII.G.S10	Maintain positive aircraft control throughout the landing using drag and braking devices, as appropriate, to come to a stop.

VIII. Postflight Procedures

Task	A. After Landing, Parking and Securing (ASEL, AMEL)
References	FAA-H-8083-2, FAA-H-8083-3; POH/AFM; AIM
Objective	To determine that the applicant exhibits satisfactory knowledge, risk management, and skills associated with normal after landing, parking, and securing procedures.
Knowledge	The applicant demonstrates understanding of:
AA.VIII.A.K1	Parking, shutdown, securing, and postflight inspection.
AA.VIII.A.K2	Documenting in-flight/postflight discrepancies.
Risk Management	The applicant demonstrates the ability to identify, assess, and mitigate risks, encompassing:
AA.VIII.A.R1	Inappropriate activities and distractions.
AA.VIII.A.R2	Confirmation or expectation bias as related to taxi instructions.
AA.VIII.A.R3	Propeller, turbofan inlet, and exhaust safety.
AA.VIII.A.R4	Airport specific security procedures.
AA.VIII.A.R5	Disembarking passengers.
Skills	The applicant demonstrates the ability to:
AA.VIII.A.S1	Demonstrate runway incursion avoidance procedures.
AA.VIII.A.S2	Comply with ATC or evaluator instructions and make radio calls as appropriate.
AA.VIII.A.S3	Coordinate with crew, if applicable, and complete the appropriate checklist(s) after clearing the runway.
AA.VIII.A.S4	Park at the gate or in an appropriate area, considering the safety of nearby persons and property.
AA.VIII.A.S5	Conduct a postflight inspection and document discrepancies and servicing requirements, if any.
AA.VIII.A.S6	Secure the airplane.

VIII. Postflight Procedures

Task	B. Seaplane Post-Landing Procedures (ASES, AMES)
References	FAA-H-8083-2, FAA-H-8083-23; POH/AFM; AIM
Objective	To determine that the applicant exhibits satisfactory knowledge, risk management, and skills associated with anchoring, docking, mooring, and ramping/beaching.
Knowledge	The applicant demonstrates understanding of:
AA.VIII.B.K1	Mooring.
AA.VIII.B.K2	Docking.
AA.VIII.B.K3	Anchoring.
AA.VIII.B.K4	Beaching/ramping.
Risk Management	The applicant demonstrates the ability to identify, assess, and mitigate risks, encompassing:
AA.VIII.B.R1	Inappropriate activities and distractions.
AA.VIII.B.R2	Confirmation or expectation bias as related to taxi instructions.
AA.VIII.B.R3	Propeller, turbofan inlet, and exhaust safety.
AA.VIII.B.R4	Airport/seaplane base security procedures.
AA.VIII.B.R5	Disembarking passengers.
Skills	The applicant demonstrates the ability to:
AA.VIII.B.S1	Comply with ATC or evaluator instructions and make radio calls as appropriate.
AA.VIII.B.S2	If anchoring, select a suitable area considering seaplane movement, water depth, tide, wind, and weather changes. Use an adequate number of anchors and lines of sufficient strength and length to ensure the seaplane's security.
AA.VIII.B.S3	If not anchoring, approach the dock/mooring buoy or beach/ramp in the proper direction and at a safe speed, considering water depth, tide, current, and wind.
AA.VIII.B.S4	Coordinate with the crew, if applicable, and complete the appropriate checklist(s).
AA.VIII.B.S5	If anchoring/mooring/beaching, secure the seaplane considering the effects of wind, waves, and changes in water level; if ramping, comply with appropriate ground movement procedures.
AA.VIII.B.S6	Conduct a postflight inspection and document discrepancies and servicing requirements, if any.

Appendix Table of Contents

Appendix 1: The Knowledge Test Eligibility, Prerequisites and Testing Centers

Knowledge Test Description

The knowledge test is an important part of the airman certification process. Applicants must pass the knowledge test before taking the practical test, when applicable.

The knowledge test consists of objective, multiple-choice questions. There is a single correct response for each test question. Each test question is independent of other questions. A correct response to one question does not depend upon, or influence, the correct response to another.

Knowledge Test Table

Test Code	Test Name	Number of Questions	Age	Allotted Time	Passing Score
ATS	Airline Transport Pilot Single-Engine Airplane	90	21	3.0	70
ATM	Airline Transport Pilot Multiengine Airplane	125	18	4.0	70
ACM	Airline Transport Pilot Multiengine Airplane Canadian Conversion	60	23	2.5	70
ASC	Airline Transport Pilot Single-Engine Airplane Canadian Conversion	40	23	2.5	70

Knowledge Test Blueprint

Airline Transport Pilot Single-Engine Airplane

ATS Knowledge Areas Required by 14 CFR part 61, section 61.155 to be on the Knowledge Test	Percentage of Test Questions
Aerodynamics	5 – 10%
Aeronautical Decision-Making	5 – 10%
Air Traffic Control Procedures	5 – 10%
Aircraft Performance	5 – 10%
Crew Resource Management (CRM)	5 – 10%
Human Factors	5 – 10%
Meteorology	10 – 15%
National Weather Service	3 – 5%
Navigation	10 – 15%
Regulations	5 – 10%
Weather / Weather Charts	10 – 15%
Weight and Balance	5 – 10%
Windshear / Turbulence	5 – 10%
Total Number of Questions	**90**

Airline Transport Pilot Multiengine Airplane

ATM Knowledge Areas Required by 14 CFR part 61, section 61.155 to be on the Knowledge Test	Percentage of Test Questions
Aerodynamics	8 – 15%
Aeronautical Decision Making	3 – 8%
Air Carrier Operations	5 – 10%
Air Traffic Control Procedures	3 – 8%
Aircraft Performance	13 – 18%
Crew Resource Management (CRM)	3 – 8%
Human Factors	3 – 8%
Leadership / Professional Development / Safety Culture	3 – 8%
Meteorology	3 – 8%
National Weather Service	3 – 5%
Navigation	10 – 15%
Regulations	10 – 15%
Weather / Weather Charts	3 – 8%
Weight and Balance	3 – 8%
Windshear / Turbulence	3 – 8%
Total Number of Questions	**125**

Aviation English Language Standard

In accordance with the requirements of 14 CFR section 61.153(b), the applicant must demonstrate the ability to read, write, speak, and understand the English language throughout the application and testing process. English language proficiency is required to communicate effectively with Air Traffic Control (ATC), to comply with ATC instructions, and to ensure clear and effective crew communication and coordination. Normal restatement of questions as would be done for a native English speaker is permitted, and does not constitute grounds for disqualification. The FAA English Language Standard (AELS) is the FAA evaluator's benchmark. It requires the applicant to demonstrate at least the ICAO level 4 standard.

Knowledge Test Requirements – Airplane Category, Single and Multiengine Class

To be eligible to take an ATP Knowledge Test, you must provide proper identification and meet the minimum age requirements in accordance with 14 CFR part 61, section 61.35. To verify your eligibility to take the test, you must provide identification that includes the applicant's:

- Photograph;
- Signature;
- Date of birth; and
- Physical, residential address.

Reference the Knowledge Testing Authorization Requirements Matrix at https://www.faa.gov/training_testing/testing/media/testing_matrix.pdffor acceptable forms of identification.

If applying for the ATP - Airplane Multiengine (ATM) test or ATP - Airplane Multiengine Canadian Conversion (ACM) test, the applicant must provide a graduation certificate from an approved provider of the ATP Certification Training Program (ATP CTP) in accordance with part 61, section 61.35.

An applicant retesting **after failure** of any ATP knowledge test is required to submit the applicable test report indicating failure, along with an endorsement from an authorized instructor who gave the applicant the required additional training in accordance with 14 CFR part 61, section 61.49. For the ATP - Airplane Multiengine (ATM) test or ATP - Airplane Multiengine Canadian Conversion (ACM) test, the authorized instructor must meet the ATP CTP instructor requirements. The endorsement must certify that the applicant is competent to pass the test.

The test proctor must retain the original failed test report presented as authorization and attach it to the applicable sign-in/out log.

Note: *For a replacement knowledge test report, see Appendix 3: Airman Knowledge Test Report.*

If an applicant seeks to add an additional category or class to an existing ATP certificate, reference 14 CFR part 61, section 61.165 for any additional knowledge test requirements.

An applicant seeking only to add an airplane type rating to an existing airman certificate in the same category and class (i.e., not adding a new category, class, or upgrading the certificate) is not required to pass a knowledge test in accordance with 14 CFR part 61, sections 61.63(d) and 61.165(e) prior to taking the practical test.

Acceptable forms of authorization for ATP Airplane Canadian Conversion (ACM and ASC) only:

- Confirmation of Verification Letter issued by FAA Airmen Certification Branch (Knowledge Testing Authorization Requirements Matrix at https://www.faa.gov/training_testing/testing/media/testing_matrix.pdf).

- Requires **no** instructor endorsement or other form of written authorization, **except** those applicants seeking a multiengine airplane ATP certificate. Those applicants are required to provide a graduation certificate from an approved provider of the ATP CTP.

Knowledge Test Centers

The FAA authorizes hundreds of knowledge testing center locations that offer a full range of airman knowledge tests. For information on authorized testing centers and to register for the knowledge test, contact one of the providers listed at www.faa.gov.

Knowledge Test Registration

When you contact a knowledge testing center to register for a test, please be prepared to select a test date, choose a testing center, and make financial arrangements for test payment when you call. You may register for test(s) several weeks in advance, and you may cancel in accordance with the testing center's cancellation policy.

Appendix 2: Knowledge Test Procedures and Tips

Before starting the actual test, the testing center will provide an opportunity to practice navigating through the test. This practice or tutorial session may include sample questions to familiarize the applicant with the look and feel of the software (e.g., selecting an answer, marking a question for later review, monitoring time remaining for the test, and other features of the testing software).

Acceptable Materials

The applicant may use the following aids, reference materials, and test materials, as long as the material does not include actual test questions or answers:

Acceptable Materials	Unacceptable Materials	Notes
Supplement book provided by proctor	Written materials that are handwritten, printed, or electronic	Testing centers may provide calculators and/or deny the use of personal calculators.
All models of aviation-oriented calculators or small electronic calculators that perform only arithmetic functions	Electronic calculators incorporating permanent or continuous type memory circuits without erasure capability.	Unit Member (proctor) may prohibit the use of your calculator if he or she is unable to determine the calculator's erasure capability
Calculators with simple programmable memories, which allow addition to, subtraction from, or retrieval of one number from the memory; or simple functions, such as square root and percentages	Magnetic Cards, magnetic tapes, modules, computer chips, or any other device upon which pre-written programs or information related to the test can be stored and retrieved	Printouts of data must be surrendered at the completion of the test if the calculator incorporates this design feature.
Scales, straightedges, protractors, plotters, navigation computers, blank log sheets, holding pattern entry aids, and electronic or mechanical calculators that are directly related to the test	Dictionaries	Before, and upon completion of the test, while in the presence of the Unit Member, actuate the ON/OFF switch or RESET button, and perform any other function that ensures erasure of any data stored in memory circuits
Manufacturer's permanently inscribed instructions on the front and back of such aids, e.g., formulas, conversions, regulations, signals, weather data, holding pattern diagrams, frequencies, weight and balance formulas, and air traffic control procedures	Any booklet or manual containing instructions related to use of test aids	Unit Member makes the final determination regarding aids, reference materials, and test materials

Test Tips

When taking a knowledge test, please keep the following points in mind:

- Carefully read the instructions provided with the test.
- Answer each question in accordance with the current regulations and guidance publications.
- Read each question carefully before looking at the answer options. You should clearly understand the problem before trying to solve it.
- After formulating a response, determine which answer option corresponds with your answer. The answer you choose should completely solve the problem.
- Remember that only one answer is complete and correct. The other possible answers are either incomplete or erroneous.

- If a certain question is difficult for you, mark it for review and return to it after you have answered the less difficult questions. This procedure will enable you to use the available time to maximum advantage.

- When solving a calculation problem, be sure to read all the associated notes.

- For questions involving use of a graph, you may request a printed copy that you can mark in computing your answer. This copy and all other notes and paperwork must be given to the testing center upon completion of the test.

Cheating or Other Unauthorized Conduct

To avoid test compromise, computer testing centers must follow strict security procedures established by the FAA and described in FAA Order 8080.6 (as amended), Conduct of Airman Knowledge Tests. The FAA has directed testing centers to terminate a test at any time a test unit member suspects that a cheating incident has occurred.

The FAA will investigate and, if the agency determines that cheating or unauthorized conduct has occurred, any airman certificate or rating you hold may be revoked. You will also be prohibited from applying for or taking any test for a certificate or rating under 14 CFR part 61 for a period of one year.

Testing Procedures for Applicants Requesting Special Accommodations

An applicant with learning or reading disability may request approval from the FAA Airman Testing Branch through the responsible Flight Standards Office or International Field Office/International Field Unit (IFO/IFU) to take an airman knowledge test using one of the three options listed below, in preferential order. Before approving any option, the Flight Standards Office or IFO/IFU inspector must advise the applicant of the regulatory certification requirement to be able to read, write, speak, and understand the English language.

Option 1: Use current testing facilities and procedures whenever possible.

Option 2: Use a self-contained, electronic device, which pronounces and displays typed-in words (e.g., the Franklin Speaking Wordmaster®) to facilitate the testing process.

> **Note:** *The device should consist of an electronic thesaurus that audibly pronounces typed-in words and presents them on a display screen. The device should also have a built-in headphone jack in order to avoid disturbing others during testing.*

Option 3: Request the proctor's assistance in reading specific words or terms from the test questions and/or supplement book. To prevent compromising the testing process, the proctor must be an individual with no aviation background or expertise. The proctor may provide reading assistance only (i.e., no explanation of words or terms). When an applicant requests this option, the Flight Standards Office or IFO/IFU inspector must contact the FAA Airman Testing Branch for assistance in selecting the test site and assisting the proctor.

Appendix 3: Airman Knowledge Test Report

Immediately upon completion of the knowledge test, the applicant receives a printed Airman Knowledge Test Report (AKTR) documenting the score with the testing center's raised, embossed seal. The applicant must retain the original AKTR. When taking the practical test, the applicant must present the original AKTR to the evaluator, who is required to assess the noted areas of deficiency during the oral portion of the practical test.

An AKTR expires 24 calendar months from the month the applicant completes the knowledge test unless it is a multiengine airplane ATP AKTR. That AKTR is valid for 60 calendar months from the month the applicant completes the knowledge test. If the AKTR expires before completion of the practical test, the applicant must retake the knowledge test unless otherwise permitted to use an expired AKTR in accordance with 14 CFR part 61, section 61.39.

To obtain a duplicate AKTR due to loss or destruction of the original, the applicant must mail a signed request accompanied by a check or money order made payable to the FAA in the amount of $12.00 to the following address:

> Federal Aviation Administration
> Airmen Certification Branch
> P.O. Box 25082
> Oklahoma City, OK 73125-0082

To obtain a copy of the application form or a list of the information required, please see the Airmen Certification Branch webpage at https://www.faa.gov/licenses_certificates/airmen_certification/test_results_replacement/

FAA Knowledge Test Question Coding

Each Task in the ACS includes an ACS code. This ACS code will soon be displayed on the AKTR to indicate what Task element was proven deficient on the knowledge test. An authorized instructor can then provide remedial training in the deficient areas and evaluators can re-test this element during the practical exam.

The ACS coding consists of four elements. For example, this code is interpreted as follows:

AA.I.B.K6:

AA	=	Applicable ACS (Airline Transport Pilot – Airplane)
I	=	Area of Operation (Preflight Preparation)
B	=	Task (Performance and Limitations)
K6	=	Knowledge Task element 6 (Effects of icing on performance.)

Knowledge test questions correspond to the ACS codes, which will ultimately replace the system of Learning Statement Codes (LSC). After this transition occurs, the Airman Knowledge Test Report (AKTR) will list an ACS code that correlates to a specific Task element for a given Area of Operation and Task. Remedial instruction and re-testing will be specific, targeted, and based on specified learning criteria. Similarly, a Notice of Disapproval for the practical test will use the ACS codes to identify the deficient Task elements. Applicants and evaluators should interpret the codes using the ACS revision in effect on the date of the knowledge test.

However, for knowledge tests taken before this system comes on line, only the LSC code (e.g., "PLT058") will be displayed on the AKTR. The LSC codes link to references and broad subject areas. By contrast, each ACS code represents a unique Task element in the ACS. Because of this fundamental difference, there is no one-to-one correlation between Learning Statement (PLT) codes and ACS codes.

Because all active knowledge test questions for the ATP – Airplane Airman Knowledge Tests now align with this ACS, evaluators can use LSC codes in conjunction with this ACS for targeting retesting of missed knowledge subject areas. The evaluator should look up the LSC code(s) on the applicant's AKTR in the Learning Statement Reference Guide at https://www.faa.gov/training_testing/testing/media/LearningStatementReferenceGuide.pdf. After noting the subject area(s), the evaluator can use the corresponding Area(s) of Operation/Task(s) in the ACS to narrow the scope of material for retesting to the appropriate ACS Area(s) of Operation and Task(s). Evaluators must verify the applicant has sufficient knowledge in those areas associated with incorrect responses on the knowledge test.

Applicant Name Considerations for the Airman Knowledge Test Report (AKTR) and the Practical Test Application Form

The applicant uses his or her full legal name on the Airman Certificate and/or Rating Application, FAA Form 8710-1, using up to 50 characters (including spaces). The applicant may exclude some middle names as necessary to meet the 50-character limit. The AKTR may not reflect the applicant's full legal name and may differ slightly from the name presented for the practical test.

If the 8710-1 shows a middle name, the AKTR may show that middle name, the correct middle initial, or no entry. The application will process correctly using the Integrated Airman Certificate and Rating Application (IACRA) system, and the Airmen Certification Branch will accept it. If an incorrect middle initial, spelling variant or different middle name is on the AKTR, or if the AKTR has a first name variation of any kind, the evaluator must attach an explanation and a scan or copy of the applicant's photo identification and attach it to the IACRA or paper application. If the last name on the AKTR has a different spelling or suffix, an IACRA application is not possible. The applicant must use a paper application, and the evaluator must include an explanation and copy of the applicant's photo identification to avoid a correction notice.

Appendix 4: The Practical Test – Eligibility and Prerequisites

The prerequisite requirements and general eligibility for a practical test and the specific requirements for the original issuance of an ATP Certificate in the airplane category can be found in 14 CFR part 61, sections 61.39 and 61.153.

There are a number of additional regulations in 14 CFR part 61 that outline requirements for an ATP certificate or the addition of an airplane type rating. Some of the key sections are highlighted below. Careful review of these sections is necessary to ensure that all of the requirements are met.

- Section 61.63 provides the endorsement and training record requirements for an applicant seeking an airplane type rating to be added to an airman certificate (other than an ATP certificate).

- Section 61.155 describes the knowledge areas for ATP applicants.

- Section 61.156 describes the training required for applicants seeking a multiengine ATP certificate.

- Section 61.157 provides the endorsement and training record requirements for an applicant seeking an airplane type rating to be added to an ATP certificate or for an airplane type rating to be concurrently completed with the original issuance of an ATP certificate.

- Section 61.159 details the aeronautical experience needed to be eligible for an ATP certificate in the airplane category.

- Section 61.160 outlines the eligibility requirements for a multiengine ATP certificate with restricted privileges with reduced aeronautical experience. It also specifies the limitations that must be placed on the ATP certificate if the applicant uses this section to qualify for the certificate.

- Section 61.165 defines the requirements for the addition of an aircraft category or class rating to an ATP certificate.

Appendix 5: Practical Test Roles, Responsibilities, and Outcomes

Applicant Responsibilities

The applicant is responsible for mastering the established standards for knowledge, risk management, and skill elements in all Tasks appropriate to the certificate and rating sought. The applicant should use this ACS, its references, and the Applicant's Checklist in this Appendix in preparation to take the practical test.

Instructor Responsibilities

The instructor, if used, is responsible for training the applicant to meet the established standards for knowledge, risk management, and skill elements in all Tasks appropriate to the certificate and rating sought. The instructor should use this ACS and its references as part of preparing the applicant to take the practical test and, if necessary, in retraining the applicant to proficiency in all subject(s) areas which were shown to be deficient by the FAA Airman Knowledge Test Report.

Evaluator Responsibilities

An evaluator[1] is:

- Aviation Safety Inspector (ASI)
- Pilot examiner (other than administrative pilot examiners);
- Training center evaluator (TCE); or
- Chief instructor, assistant chief instructor or check instructor of a pilot school holding examining authority.

The evaluator who conducts the practical test is responsible for determining that the applicant meets the established standards of aeronautical knowledge, risk management, and skills (flight proficiency), and for each Task in the appropriate ACS. This responsibility also includes verifying the experience requirements specified for a certificate or rating and training requirements for an aircraft type rating.

Prior to beginning the practical test, the evaluator must also determine that the applicant meets the FAA Aviation English Language Proficiency Standard. An applicant for an FAA certificate or rating should be able to communicate in English in a discernible and understandable manner with ATC, pilots, and others involved in preparing an aircraft for flight and operating an aircraft in flight. This communication may or may not involve the use of the radio. An applicant for an FAA certificate issued in accordance with part 61, 63, 65, or 107 who cannot hear or speak due to a medical deficiency may be eligible for an FAA certificate with specific operational limitations. For additional guidance, reference AC 60-28, FAA English Language Standard for an FAA Certificate issued Under 14 CFR Parts 61, 63, 65, and 107, as amended.

The evaluator must develop a scenario-based Plan of Action (POA), written in English, to conduct the practical test. The POA must include all of the required Areas of Operation and Tasks and should be scenario-based as much as practical. As a scenario unfolds during the test, the evaluator will introduce problems and emergencies that the applicant must manage. The evaluator has the discretion to modify the POA in order to accommodate unexpected situations as they arise.

In the integrated ACS framework, the Areas of Operation contain Tasks that include "knowledge" elements (such as K1), "risk management" elements (such as R1), and "skill" elements (such as S1). Knowledge and risk management elements are primarily evaluated during the knowledge testing phase of the airman certification process. The evaluator must assess the applicant on all skill elements for each Task included in each Area of Operation of the ACS, unless otherwise noted. The evaluator administering the practical test has the discretion to combine Tasks/elements as appropriate to testing scenarios.

---

[1] An evaluator that conducts ATP certificate evaluations in accordance with an approved part 121 or part 135 training and checking program is not required to use this document.

The required minimum elements to include in the POA from each applicable Task, unless otherwise noted within a specific Task, are as follows:

- At least one knowledge element;

- At least one risk management element;

- All skill elements unless otherwise noted; and

- Any Task elements in which the applicant was shown to be deficient on the knowledge test, if a knowledge test is required.

Note: *Task elements added to the POA on the basis of being listed on the AKTR may satisfy the other minimum Task element requirements. The missed items on the AKTR are not required to be added in addition to the minimum Task element requirements.*

There is no expectation for testing every knowledge and risk management element in a Task, but the evaluator has discretion to sample as needed to ensure the applicant's mastery of that Task.

Unless otherwise noted in the Task, the evaluator must test each item in the skills section by asking the applicant to perform each one. As safety of flight conditions permit, the evaluator may use questions during flight to test knowledge and risk management elements not evident in the demonstrated skills. To the greatest extent practicable, evaluators shall test the applicant's ability to apply and correlate information, and use rote questions only when they are appropriate for the material being tested. If the Task includes sub-elements, the evaluator may select an appropriate sub-element (e.g., AA.I.B.K3f – Weight and balance). Tasks requiring evaluation of more than one sub-element are annotated accordingly. If the broader primary element is selected, the evaluator must develop questions only from material covered in the references listed for the Task.

Possible Outcomes of the Test

There are three possible outcomes of an evaluation event for an initial ATP certificate or added rating: (1) Temporary Airman Certificate (satisfactory), (2) Notice of Disapproval (unsatisfactory), or (3) Letter of Discontinuance.

If the evaluator determines that a Task is incomplete, or the outcome is uncertain, the evaluator may require the applicant to repeat that Task, or portions of that Task. This provision does not mean that instruction, practice, or the repetition of an unsatisfactory Task is permitted during the practical test.

If the outcome is unsatisfactory, the evaluator must issue a Notice of Disapproval.

Satisfactory Performance

In accordance with 14 CFR section 61.43, satisfactory performance requires that the applicant:

- Demonstrate the Tasks specified in the Areas of Operation for the certificate or rating sought within the established standards;

- Demonstrate mastery of the aircraft by performing each Task successfully;

- Demonstrate proficiency and competency in accordance with the approved standards;

- Demonstrate sound judgment and exercise aeronautical decision-making/risk management; and

Depending upon the pilot flight crew complement required for the test, the pilot is expected to demonstrate competence in crew resource management in an operation or airplane certificated for more than one required pilot crewmember, or single-pilot competence in an operation or airplane that is certificated for single-pilot operations.

Satisfactory performance will result in the issuance of a temporary certificate or the continuation or reinstatement of an operating privilege, as appropriate to the checking event being completed.

If a successful check is conducted under an operator's approved training and checking program, it is considered to have met the flight proficiency requirements of 14 CFR part 61, section 61.157 for the issuance of an ATP certificate and an appropriate rating.

Unsatisfactory Performance

Typical areas of unsatisfactory performance and grounds for disqualification include:

- Any action or lack of action by the applicant that requires corrective intervention by the evaluator to maintain safe flight.
- Failure to use proper and effective visual scanning techniques to clear the area before and while performing maneuvers.
- Consistently exceeding tolerances stated in the skill elements of the Task.
- Failure to take prompt corrective action when tolerances are exceeded.
- Failure to exercise risk management.

If, in the judgment of the evaluator, the applicant does not meet the standards for any Task, the applicant fails the Task and associated Area of Operation. The test is unsatisfactory, and the evaluator issues a Notice of Disapproval. The evaluator lists the Area(s) of Operation in which the applicant did not meet the standard, any Area(s) of Operation not tested, and the number of practical test failures. The evaluator should also list the Tasks failed or Tasks not tested within any unsatisfactory or partially completed Area(s) of Operation. If the applicant's inability to meet English language requirements contributed to the failure of a Task, the evaluator must note "English Proficiency" on the Notice of Disapproval.

The evaluator or the applicant may end the test if the applicant fails a Task. The evaluator may continue the test only with the consent of the applicant. The applicant is entitled to credit only for those Areas of Operation and the associated Tasks performed satisfactorily.

Discontinuance

When it is necessary to discontinue a practical test for reasons other than unsatisfactory performance (e.g., equipment failure, weather, illness), the evaluator must return all test paperwork to the applicant. The evaluator must prepare, sign, and issue a Letter of Discontinuance that lists those Areas of Operation the applicant successfully completed and the time period remaining to complete the test. The evaluator should advise the applicant to present the Letter of Discontinuance to the evaluator when the practical test resumes in order to receive credit for the items successfully completed. The Letter of Discontinuance becomes part of the applicant's certification file.

Testing Date Limits

If all increments of the practical test are not completed on the same date, then all of the remaining increments of the test must be completed within two calendar months after the month the applicant began the test.[2] Following a discontinuance or an unsatisfactory performance, an applicant may receive credit for items passed, but only within the 60 days after the date of a first failure or Letter of Discontinuance.[3] While an applicant may receive credit for any Task(s) successfully completed within a failed or partially tested Area of Operation, the evaluator has discretion to reevaluate any Task(s). When an applicant is entitled to credit for Areas of Operation previously passed as indicated on a Notice of Disapproval or Letter of Discontinuance, evaluators should continue using the PTS/ACS effective on the test cycle start date.

---

[2] 14 CFR part 61, section 61.39(f)
[3] 14 CFR part 61, section 61.43(f)

Practical Test Checklist (Applicant)
Appointment with Evaluator

Evaluator's Name: _____

Location: _____

Date/Time: _____

Note: Applicability of each item is contingent on the aircraft or Flight Simulation Training Device used.

Acceptable Aircraft

- ☐ Aircraft Documents:
    - ☐ Airworthiness Certificate
    - ☐ Registration Certificate
    - ☐ Operating Limitations
- ☐ Aircraft Maintenance Records:
    - ☐ Logbook Record of Airworthiness Inspections and AD Compliance
- ☐ Pilot's Operating Handbook, FAA-Approved Aircraft Flight Manual

Personal Equipment

- ☐ View-Limiting Device
- ☐ Current Aeronautical Charts (printed or electronic)
- ☐ Computer and Plotter
- ☐ Flight Plan Form
- ☐ Flight Logs (printed or electronic)
- ☐ Chart Supplements, Airport Diagrams, and Appropriate Publications
- ☐ Current AIM

Personal Records

- ☐ Identification—Photo/Signature ID
- ☐ Pilot Certificate
- ☐ Current Medical Certificate or BasicMed qualification (when applicable)
- ☐ Completed FAA Form 8710-1, Airman Certificate and/or Rating Application with Instructor's Signature or completed IACRA form
- ☐ Applicant FAA Tracking Number (FTN) if 8710-1 completed via IACRA
- ☐ Original Airman Knowledge Test Report
- ☐ Pilot Logbook with appropriate Instructor Endorsements
- ☐ FAA Form 8060-5, Notice of Disapproval (if applicable)
- ☐ Letter of Discontinuance (if applicable)
- ☐ Approved School Graduation Certificate (if applicable)
- ☐ Original ATP CTP Graduation Certificate (if applicable)
- ☐ Evaluator's Fee (if applicable)

Initial ATP Certificate Task Table

Each column title in the table below identifies the *ATP class rating sought on the initial ATP certificate*. The evaluator must evaluate the applicant in the Areas of Operation and Tasks listed in the table below.

Areas of Operation	ASEL*	ASES*	AMEL**	AMES**
I	A,B,C,F,G	A,B,C,F,G,H	A,B,C,D,E,F,G	All
II	A,B,C,E	A,B,D,E	A,B,C,E	A,B,D,E
III	A,B,I,J	All	A,B,I,J	All
IV	All	All	All	All
V	All	All	All	All
VI	All	All	All	All
VII	A,B,C,G	A,B,C,G	A,B,D,E,F,G	A,B,D,E,F,G
VIII	A	B	A	B

*An applicant seeking an ATP certificate in the airplane category with a single-engine class rating (ASEL or ASES) must demonstrate additional Tasks if the applicant meets any of the following criteria[4]:

- An applicant with pilot privileges for single-engine airplanes who has not completed a commercial practical test in a single-engine airplane and is seeking an ATP certificate with an airplane single-engine class rating must perform the Power-Off 180° Accuracy Approach and Landing Task in accordance with the Commercial Pilot – Airplane ACS (FAA-S-ACS-7 as amended), Area of Operation IV, Task M. (Ref. 14 CFR part 61, sections 61.153 and 61.165(b) and (e))

- An applicant that does not hold an airman certificate with an airplane single-engine class rating, who is seeking an ATP certificate with an airplane single-engine class rating, must perform both the Forward Slip to the Landing Task in accordance with the Private Pilot – Airplane ACS (FAA-S-ACS-6 as amended), Area of Operation IV, Task M and a Power-Off 180° Accuracy Approach and Landing Task, Commercial Pilot – Airplane ACS (FAA-S-ACS-7 as amended), Area of Operation IV, Task M. (Ref. 14 CFR part 61, sections 61.153 and 61.165(b) and (e))

**If an applicant for an ATP certificate in the airplane category, multiengine class rating (AMEL or AMES) does not hold an airplane multiengine class rating on his or her current pilot certificate, or current airplane multiengine rating or multiengine type rating on a foreign license, the pilot must perform the Maneuvering with One Engine Inoperative Task and the V_{MC} Demonstration Task in accordance with the Commercial Pilot – Airplane ACS (FAA-S-ACS-7 as amended), Area of Operation X, Tasks A and B.

Task Tables for Adding a Rating to an ATP Certificate

For an applicant who holds an ATP certificate and seeks an additional airplane category and/or class rating at the ATP level, the evaluator must evaluate that applicant in the Areas of Operation and Tasks listed in the Additional Rating Task Table appropriate to the rating sought.

If the applicant holds an ATP certificate with two or more category or class ratings, and the ratings table indicates differing required Tasks, the "least restrictive" entry applies. For example, if "All" and "None" are indicated for one Area of Operation, the "None" entry applies. If "B" and "B, C" are indicated, the "B entry applies.

To add a single-engine class rating (ASEL or ASES), the applicant must demonstrate additional Tasks if the applicant meets any of the following criteria:

- An applicant with pilot privileges for single-engine airplanes who has not completed a commercial practical test in a single-engine airplane and is seeking an ATP certificate with an airplane single-engine

---

[4] The applicant in these situations would be meeting the eligibility requirements of 14 CFR section 61.153 with qualifications other than a commercial pilot certificate in the airplane category and a single-engine class rating. Note the requirement to hold a commercial pilot certificate and an instrument rating is not category specific.

class rating must perform the Power-Off 180° Accuracy Approach and Landing Task in accordance with the Commercial Pilot – Airplane ACS (FAA-S-ACS-7 as amended), Area of Operation IV, Task M. (Ref. 14 CFR part 61, sections 61.153 and 61.165(b) and (e))

- An applicant that does not hold an airman certificate with an airplane single-engine class rating, who is seeking an ATP certificate with an airplane single-engine class rating, must perform both the Forward Slip to the Landing Task in accordance with the Private Pilot – Airplane ACS (FAA-S-ACS-6 as amended), Area of Operation IV, Task M and a Power-Off 180° Accuracy Approach and Landing Task, Commercial Pilot – Airplane ACS (FAA-S-ACS-7 as amended), Area of Operation IV, Task M. (Ref. sections 61.153 and 61.165(b) and (e))

To add a multiengine class rating (AMEL or AMES) when the applicant does not hold an airplane multiengine class rating on his or her current pilot certificate, or current airplane multiengine rating or multiengine type rating on a foreign license, the pilot must perform the Maneuvering with One Engine Inoperative Task and the V_{MC} Demonstration Task in accordance with the Commercial Pilot – Airplane ACS (FAA-S-ACS-7 as amended), Area of Operation X, Tasks A and B.

Addition of a Class Rating to an existing ATP Certificate

Each column title in the tables below identifies the *ATP pilot ratings held on the existing certificate*. Required Tasks are indicated by either the Task letter(s) that apply(s) or an indication that all or none of the Tasks must be tested based on the corresponding row for each Area of Operation.

Tasks Required for the Addition of an Airplane Single-Engine Land Class Rating (ASEL)

Areas of Operation	ASES	AMEL	AMES	RH
I	A,B	A,B	A,B	A,B
II	A,C,E	A,E	A,C,E	A,B,C,E
III	A,B,I	A,B	A,B,I	A,B,I,J
IV	C	C	C	All
V	None	None	None	All
VI	None	None	None	All
VII	A,B,C,G	A,B,C,G	A,B,C,G	A,B,C,G
VIII	A	None	A	A

Tasks Required for the Addition of an Airplane Single-Engine Sea Class Rating (ASES)

Areas of Operation	ASEL	AMEL	AMES	RH
I	A,B,H	A,B,H	A,B	A,B,H
II	A,B,D,E	A,B,D,E	A,E	A,B,D,E
III	A,B,C,D,E,F,G,H,I	A,B,C,D,E,F,G,H,I	A,B,I	All
IV	C	C	C	All
V	None	None	None	All
VI	None	None	None	All
VII	A,B,C,G	A,B,C,G	A,B,C,G	A,B,C,G
VIII	B	B	None	B

Tasks Required for the Addition of an Airplane Multiengine Land Class Rating (AMEL)

Areas of Operation	ASEL	ASES	AMES	RH
I	A,B,D,E	A,B,D,E	A,B	A,B,C,D,E,F,G
II	A,B,E	A,B,C,E	A,B,C,E	A,B,C,E
III	A,B,I	A,B,I	A,B,I	A,B,I,J
IV	All	All	C	All
V	All	All	None	All
VI	None	None	None	All
VII	A,B,D,E,F,G	A,B,D,E,F,G	A,B,E,G	A,B,D,E,F,G
VIII	A	A	A	A

Tasks Required for the Addition of an Airplane Multiengine Sea Class Rating (AMES)

Areas of Operation	AMEL*	ASEL	ASES	RH
I	A,B,H	A,B,D,E,H	A,B,D,E,H	All
II	A,B,D,E	A,B,D,E	A,B,D,E	A,B,D,E
III	A,B,C,D,E,F,G,H,I	A,B,C,D,E,F,G,H,I	A,B,I	All
IV	C	All	C	All
V	None	All	All	All
VI	None	A,G,H	None	All
VII	A,B,E,G	A,B,D,E,F,G	A,B,D,E,F,G	A,B,D,E,F,G
VIII	B	B	B	B

*When adding the Airplane Multiengine Sea Rating (AMES) to an existing ATP Airplane Multiengine Land (AMEL) Certificate, any Task requiring the feathering of propellers may be simulated. The applicant is not required to supply a seaplane with propeller feathering capability.

Addition of a Type Rating to an Existing Pilot Certificate

In accordance with 14 CFR part 61, sections 61.63 and 61.157, an applicant may add a type rating to an existing pilot certificate. The following table identifies the Tasks required for the category and class of type rating sought. Each column title *identifies the class of the type rating sought on an existing pilot certificate*. There is no Task credit available for applicants that hold a pilot type rating issued in accordance with section 61.55.

Areas of Operation	ASEL	AMEL	ASES	AMES
I	A,B	A,B	A,B,H	A,B,H
II	A,B,C,E	A,B,C,E	A,B,D,E	A,B,D,E
III	A,B,I,J	A,B,I,J	All	All
IV	All	All	All	All
V	All	All	All	All
VI	All	All	All	All
VII	A,B,C,G	A,B,D,E,F,G	A,B,C,G	A,B,D,E,F,G
VIII	A	A	B	B

Note: Available type ratings can be located at: http://registry.faa.gov/TypeRatings/Type_Rating_Table.pdf.

Addition of a VFR Only Type Rating to an Existing Pilot Certificate

In accordance with section 61.63(e) or section 61.157(g), as applicable, an applicant may add a type rating to a pilot certificate with an airplane that is not capable of instrument flight and therefore completion of the applicable Tasks by reference to instruments is not possible. This results in a "VFR only" limitation to be added to the type rating on the pilot certificate. The following table identifies the Tasks required for the category and class of type rating sought. Each column title *identifies the class of the type rating sought on an existing pilot certificate*.

Areas of Operation	AMEL	ASEL	AMES	ASES
I	A,B	A,B	A,B,H	A,B,H
II	A,B,C,E	A,B,C,E	A,B,D,E	A,B,D,E
III	A,B,I,J	A,B,I,J	All	All
IV	All	All	All	All
V	All	All	All	All
VI	None	None	None	None
VII	A,B,D,E,G	A,B,C,G	A,B,D,E,G	A,B,C,G
VIII	A	A	B	B

Note: Any Task that is normally required to be performed by reference to instruments would be conducted using visual references for the purposes of a VFR type rating.

Removal of the "Second-In-Command Required" Limitation from a Type Rating

A pilot, who holds an airplane type rating with a "Second-In-Command Required" Limitation, may be tested to remove the limitation and be issued an unrestricted type rating. The practical test to remove the restriction does not require evaluation of all Areas of Operation and Tasks as a single-pilot. The practical test is conducted in accordance with the Airline Transport Pilot and Type Rating for Airplane ACS (FAA-S-ACS-11 as amended), and the pilot must demonstrate single-pilot competency in the following Areas of Operation and Tasks listed below.

Areas of Operation	AMEL Tasks	AMES Tasks
I	None	None
II	A,B,C,E	A,B,D,E
III	A,B,I,J	All
IV	B,C	B,C
V	None	None
VI	All	All
VII	A,B,D,E,F,G	A,B,D,E,F,G
VIII	A	B

Circle-to-Land Limitation on an ATP Certificate or Type Rating

A pilot may receive a circle-to-land limitation through an approved air carrier training and checking program restricting a circling approach in the specified airplane type to visual meteorological conditions (VMC) only. An example of the certificate notation would be: "CL-65 CIRC APCH VMC ONLY." This restriction may be removed when the applicant receives training in the circling maneuver in the same type of airplane for which he or she has the limitation and satisfactorily demonstrates a circling approach and landing in that same airplane type with an appropriately qualified evaluator.

If as part of the approved air carrier training and checking program a pilot's initial ATP certificate is issued concurrently with an airplane type rating and the circling maneuver is not checked, the ATP certificate would also have a circling limitation. For example, the certificate notation would be: "ATP CIRC APCH VMC ONLY, CL-65 CIRC APCH VMC ONLY." This restriction may be removed from the ATP certificate upon completion of an evaluation of the circling maneuver tasks in an airplane representative of the class held on the applicant's ATP certificate. The airplane used does not have to be type-specific, but should reflect a class of airplane for which the pilot has ATP privileges. Depending upon the airplane used, training may be required. The applicant must satisfactorily demonstrate a circling approach and landing to an appropriately qualified evaluator. However, if a CL-65 was not used for the circling evaluation, the limitation would be removed from the ATP certificate only and would remain for the CL-65 type rating. Removal of that limitation would require demonstration of the circling maneuver in type as described in the previous paragraph.

Airline Transport Pilot/Type Rating for Airplane ACS (FAA-S-ACS-11 as amended)

Area of Operation	Tasks
VI	G, H

Airplane Multiengine Land Limited to Center Thrust

A center thrust limitation for the AMEL rating is issued to applicants who complete the practical test for the AMEL rating in an aircraft that does not have a manufacturer's published V_{MC}.

When conducting a practical test for a pilot that has not previously demonstrated competence in a multiengine airplane with a published V_{MC}, or when removing the center thrust limitation from the AMEL rating, the applicant must be tested on the following Areas of Operation and Tasks from the Airline Transport Pilot and Type Rating for Airplane ACS (FAA-S-ACS-11 as amended) and Commercial Pilot – Airplane ACS (FAA-S-ACS-7 as amended) in a multiengine airplane that has a manufacturer's published V_{MC} speed. This speed can be found on the type certificate data sheet (TCDS) or in the AFM. If the limitation will be removed under part 121, 135, or 142, it must be done in accordance with an approved curriculum or training program.

Airline Transport Pilot/Type Rating for Airplane ACS (FAA-S-ACS-11 as amended)

Areas of Operation	Tasks
III	I
VII	B,D,E

Commercial Pilot – Airplane ACS (FAA-S-ACS-7 as amended)

Area of Operation	Tasks
X	A,B

Appendix 6: Safety of Flight

General

Safety of flight must be the prime consideration at all times. The evaluator, applicant, and crew must be constantly alert for other traffic. If performing aspects of a given maneuver, such as emergency procedures, would jeopardize safety, the evaluator will ask the applicant to simulate that portion of the maneuver. The evaluator will assess the applicant's use of visual scanning and collision avoidance procedures throughout the flight portion of the test.

Stall and Spin Awareness

During flight training and testing, the applicant and the instructor or evaluator must always recognize and avoid operations that could lead to an inadvertent stall or spin and inadvertent loss of control.

Use of Checklists

Throughout the practical test, the applicant is evaluated on the use of an appropriate checklist.

Assessing proper checklist use depends upon the specific Task. In all cases, the evaluator should determine whether the applicant demonstrates CRM, appropriately divides attention, and uses proper visual scanning. In some abnormal or emergency situations, reading the actual checklist or other published procedure may be impractical or unsafe. In such cases, the evaluator should assess the applicant's performance of immediate action "memory" items along with his or her review of the appropriate checklist or other published procedure once conditions permit.

In a single-pilot airplane, the applicant should demonstrate Single Pilot Resource Management (SRM). Proper use is dependent on the specific Task being evaluated. The situation may be such that the use of the checklist while accomplishing elements of an Objective would be either unsafe or impractical in a single-pilot operation. In this case, a review of the checklist after the elements have been accomplished is appropriate.

Use of Distractions

Numerous studies indicate that many accidents have occurred when the pilot has been distracted during critical phases of flight. The evaluator should incorporate realistic distractions during the flight portion of the practical test to evaluate the pilot's situational awareness and ability to utilize proper control technique while dividing attention both inside and outside the cockpit.

Positive Exchange of Flight Controls

There must always be a clear understanding of who has control of the aircraft. Prior to flight, the pilots involved should conduct a briefing that includes reviewing the procedures for exchanging flight controls.

The FAA recommends a positive three-step process for exchanging flight controls between pilots:

- When one pilot seeks to have the other pilot take control of the aircraft, he or she will say, "You have the flight controls."

- The second pilot acknowledges immediately by saying, "I have the flight controls."

- The first pilot again says, "You have the flight controls," and visually confirms the exchange.

Pilots should follow this procedure during any exchange of flight controls, including any occurrence during the practical test. The FAA also recommends that both pilots use a visual check to verify that the exchange has occurred. There must never be any doubt as to who is flying the aircraft.

Aeronautical Decision-Making, Risk Management, Crew Resource Management, and Single-Pilot Resource Management

Throughout the practical test, the evaluator must assess the applicant's ability to use sound aeronautical decision-making procedures in order to identify hazards and mitigate risk. The evaluator must accomplish this requirement by reference to the risk management elements of the given Task(s), and by developing scenarios that incorporate and combine Tasks appropriate to assessing the applicant's risk management in making safe aeronautical decisions. For example, the evaluator may develop a scenario that incorporates weather decisions and performance planning.

In assessing the applicant's performance in all Tasks in this practical test standard, the evaluator should take note of the applicant's use of CRM or SRM, as applicable. CRM/SRM is the set of competencies that includes situational awareness, communication skills, teamwork, task allocation, and decision-making within a comprehensive framework of standard operating procedures (SOPs). SRM specifically refers to the management of all resources onboard the aircraft as well as outside resources available to the single pilot. Resources a pilot may involve in decisions as part of CRM/SRM include dispatchers, flight attendants, maintenance personnel, flight operations managers, and air traffic control.

Deficiencies in CRM/SRM often contribute to the unsatisfactory performance of a Task. While evaluation of CRM/SRM may appear to be somewhat subjective, the evaluator should use the risk management elements of the given Task(s) to determine whether the applicant's performance of the Task(s) demonstrates both understanding and application of the associated risk management elements.

If the evaluator, other than an FAA Inspector, is qualified as a safety pilot and current in the specific make and model aircraft certified for two or more crewmembers, he or she may occupy a duty position. If the evaluator occupies a duty position on an aircraft that requires two or more crewmembers, the evaluator must fulfill the duties of that position. Moreover, when occupying a required duty position, the evaluator must perform CRM functions as briefed and requested by the applicant except during the accomplishment of steep turns and approach to stalls. During these two Tasks the applicant must demonstrate their ability to control the aircraft without the intervention from the pilot monitoring. However, for aircraft requiring only one pilot, the evaluator may not assist the applicant in the management of the aircraft, radio communications, tuning and identifying navigational equipment, or using navigation charts.

Multiengine Airplane Considerations

For safety reasons, when the practical test is conducted in an airplane, the applicant must perform Tasks that require powerplant shutdown or propeller feathering only under conditions and at a position and altitude where it is possible to make a safe landing on an established airport if there is difficulty in restarting the powerplant or unfeathering the propeller. The evaluator must select an entry altitude that will allow the Powerplant Failure Tasks to be completed no lower than 3,000 feet AGL or the manufacturer's recommended altitude, whichever is higher. If it is not possible to restart the powerplant or unfeather the propeller while airborne, the applicant and the evaluator should treat the situation as an emergency.

At altitudes lower than 3,000 feet AGL, powerplant failure should be simulated as recommended by the manufacturer. For propeller-driven airplanes, powerplant failure should be simulated by reducing throttle to idle and then establishing zero thrust. For additional Task considerations, see Appendix 7: Aircraft, Equipment, and Operational Requirements & Limitations, Area of Operation III, Takeoffs and Landings, Task I. Rejected Takeoff, and the powerplant failure Tasks in Area of Operation VII. Emergency Operations.

Except for a type rating practical test, for an airplane equipped with propellers (including turboprop), the applicant must feather one propeller and shut down an engine unless the manufacturer prohibits it. However, if an applicant has not previously demonstrated multiengine airplane tasks for the commercial pilot certificate, the applicant cannot use a propeller-equipped airplane where the manufacturer prohibits feathering for the initial ATP multiengine airplane certificate. If the practical test is conducted in an airplane that requires the pilot to hold a type rating, the applicant may perform a simulated powerplant failure. In all other cases, the applicant must feather and unfeather the propeller while airborne.

Practical tests conducted in an FSTD can only be accomplished as part of an approved curriculum or training program. Any limitations on powerplant failure will be noted in that program. In addition, an evaluator may reference an airplane's FSB report, which may include other safety related considerations for performing specific tasks.

Single-Engine Airplane Considerations

For safety reasons, the evaluator will not simulate a powerplant failure in a single-engine airplane unless it is possible to safely complete a landing.

For airplanes that have an FSB Report, reference it for any other safety related considerations in performing specific tasks.

High Performance Aircraft Considerations

In some high performance airplanes, the power setting may have to be reduced below the suggested power setting in this ACS to prevent excessively high pitch attitudes greater than 30° nose up.

Appendix 7: Aircraft, Equipment, and Operational Requirements & Limitations

Aircraft Requirements & Limitations

14 CFR part 61, section 61.45 prescribes the required aircraft and equipment for a practical test. The regulation states the minimum aircraft registration and airworthiness requirements as well as the minimum equipment requirements, to include the minimum required controls.

Multiengine practical tests require normal engine shutdowns and restarts in the air, to include propeller feathering and unfeathering. The Airplane Flight Manual (AFM) must not prohibit these procedures, but low power settings for cooling periods prior to the actual shutdown in accordance with the AFM are acceptable and encouraged. For a type rating in an airplane not certificated with inflight unfeathering capability, a simulated powerplant failure is acceptable.

If the multiengine airplane used for the practical test does not publish a V_{MC}, then the center thrust limitation will be added to the certificate issued from this check, unless the applicant has previously demonstrated competence in a multiengine airplane with a published V_{MC}.

If the aircraft presented for the practical test has inoperative instruments or equipment, it must be addressed in accordance with 14 CFR part 91, section 91.213. If the aircraft can be operated in accordance with 14 CFR part 91, section 91.213, then it must be determined if the inoperative instruments or equipment are required to complete the practical test.

For a type rating or experimental aircraft authorization in an aircraft covered under the FAA's Specialty Aircraft Examiner (SAE) program, the evaluator has discretion to omit any skill element(s) deemed unsuitable or unsafe for the operational or performance characteristics of the aircraft, provided that such determinations are coordinated with the Specialty Aircraft Examiner Branch.

Equipment Requirements & Limitations

The aircraft must meet the requirements as outlined in 14 CFR part 61, section 61.45.

To assist in management of the aircraft during the practical test, the applicant is expected to demonstrate automation management skills by utilizing installed, available, or airborne equipment such as autopilot, avionics and systems displays, and/or a flight management system (FMS). The evaluator is expected to test the applicant's knowledge of the systems that are installed and operative during both the oral and flight portions of the practical test. If the applicant has trained using a portable EFB to display charts and data, and wishes to use the EFB during the practical test, the applicant is expected to demonstrate appropriate knowledge, risk management, and skill.

If the practical test is conducted in an aircraft, the applicant is required by 14 CFR part 61, section 61.45(d)(2) to provide an appropriate view limiting device acceptable to the evaluator. The applicant and the evaluator should establish a procedure as to when and how this device should be used, and brief this procedure before the flight. The device must be used during all testing that requires flight "solely by reference to instruments." This device must prevent the applicant from having visual reference outside the aircraft, but it must not restrict the evaluator's ability to see and avoid other traffic. The use of a view-limiting device does not apply to specific elements within a Task when there is a requirement for visual references.

If a type rating practical test is given in an amphibious airplane, the type rating must bear the limitation "Limited to Land" or "Limited to Sea," as appropriate, unless the applicant demonstrates proficiency in both land and sea operations.

Operational Requirements, Limitations, & Task Information

The applicant must perform the tasks in Areas of Operation IV through VII in actual or simulated instrument conditions, except for:

a. Testing of elements that require visual maneuvering; or

b. When the aircraft's type certificate makes the aircraft incapable of operating under instrument flight rules (IFR). See Appendix 5: Practical Test Roles, Responsibilities, and Outcomes for required Tasks to be completed for a VFR Only type rating.

I. Preflight Preparation

Task A. Operation of Systems

This Task is required for all certificates, ratings, and type ratings. The "Equipment Examination" from the superseded testing standard has been incorporated into this task. The focus on systems knowledge for the ATP certificate and the type rating is on the airplane brought to the test. The knowledge elements in Task A. include a broad categorization of airplane systems. Within each element are examples of the content that the evaluator could ask about, but the questions should reflect the airplane brought for the practical test. Although the examples are comprehensive, they are not necessarily all-inclusive. The explanation of an airplane's systems and components should be part of the oral portion of the practical test.

The ACS is structured so that certain Skill elements in Task A. may be assessed during the oral portion of the practical test. The Skill elements test an applicant's systems knowledge based upon the airplane provided in order to adequately evaluate the applicant's knowledge, understanding, and skill for the specific airplane systems, its components, checklists, and procedures.

Task B. Performance and Limitations

This Task is required for all certificates, ratings, and type ratings. When a practical test does not require a knowledge test, the evaluator selects at least one Knowledge element and should tailor the questions towards the actual airplane provided for the practical test. If the applicant was required to pass a knowledge test and missed any Knowledge elements for Task B., the evaluator may ask general or airplane specific questions on performance charts, performance calculations, and factors that affect airplane performance.

The ACS is structured so that certain Skill elements in Task B. may be assessed during the oral portion of the practical test. The Skill elements test an applicant's knowledge and understanding of airplane performance and the ability to calculate weight and balance specific to the airplane provided.

Task C. Weather Information (ATP)

This task is only required for applicants seeking an initial ATP certificate in accordance with section 61.155. Additional ratings added to an ATP certificate or type ratings added to a pilot certificate do not require completion of this task. Any risk assessment tool is acceptable provided the applicant is able to assess and mitigate risks.

Task D. High Altitude Aerodynamics (ATP) (AMEL, AMES)

This task is only required for applicants seeking an initial ATP certificate in the multiengine class in accordance with section 61.155. The specific content in this task is included in the training required for multiengine applicants in accordance with section 61.156 regardless of the multiengine airplane brought for the practical test. This task is not required for applicants seeking an ATP certificate with a single-engine class rating (initial or add-on) or applicants adding a single-engine airplane type rating to a pilot certificate.

Task E. Air Carrier Operations (ATP) (AMEL, AMES)

This task is only required for applicants seeking an initial ATP certificate in the multiengine class in accordance with section 61.155. The specific content in this task is included in the training required for multiengine applicants in accordance with section 61.156 regardless of the multiengine airplane brought for the practical test. This task is not required for applicants seeking an ATP certificate with a single-engine class rating (initial or add-on) or applicants adding a single-engine airplane type rating to a pilot certificate.

Task F. Human Factors (ATP)

This task is only required for applicants seeking an initial ATP certificate in accordance with 14 CFR part 61, section 61.155. Additional ratings added to an ATP certificate or type ratings added to a pilot certificate do not require completion of this task. The ability to perform a self-assessment and determine fitness for flight is also applicable to practical tests given in an FSTD.

Task G. The Code of Federal Regulations (ATP)

This task is only required for applicants seeking an initial ATP certificate in accordance with 14 CFR part 61, section 61.155. Additional ratings added to an ATP certificate or type ratings added to a pilot certificate do not require completion of this Task. The evaluator has the discretion to choose a representative sampling of one or more rule parts. Although an applicant may not be employed by an air carrier, a single-engine airplane knowledge test will cover part 135. Similarly, a multiengine airplane knowledge test will cover parts 117 and 121. An applicant is required to know the relevant subparts listed in the elements applicable to the test taken.

II. Preflight Procedures

Task A. Preflight Assessment

The preflight inspection of the airplane, part of Area of Operation II, Task A should be completed prior to all other portions of the preflight assessment, and must be completed prior to the flight portion of the practical test. For testing, use of an airplane to conduct a preflight inspection is preferred; however, a pictorial aircraft preflight inspection program using courseware may be authorized for testing in a part 142 training curriculum. Such an approval would only apply to pilots adding a type rating.

If a flight engineer is a required crewmember for a particular type airplane, the actual visual inspection may be waived. The actual visual inspection may be replaced by using an approved pictorial means that realistically portrays the location and detail of inspection items. On airplanes requiring a flight engineer, an applicant must demonstrate satisfactory knowledge of the flight engineer functions for the safe completion of the flight if the flight engineer becomes ill or incapacitated during a flight.

Task B. Powerplant Start

For practical tests in an airplane, an applicant's ability to respond to a powerplant start failure or malfunction can be assessed through scenario-based oral questioning.

Task E. Before Takeoff Checks

Each applicant must give a briefing before each takeoff. If the operator or aircraft manufacturer has not specified a briefing, the briefing must cover the items appropriate for the conditions, such as: departure runway, departure procedure, power settings, speeds, abnormal or emergency procedures prior to or after reaching decision speed (i.e., V_1 or V_{MC}), emergency return intentions, and what is expected of the other crewmembers during the takeoff/departure. If the first takeoff briefing is satisfactory, the evaluator may allow the applicant to brief only the changes, during the remainder of the flight.

III. Takeoffs and Landings

The applicant must make at least three actual landings with at least one to a full stop. Landing Tasks may be combined where appropriate. This includes the Landing Tasks found in the Instrument Procedures Area of Operation and the Emergency Operations Area of Operation.

Briefings

Each applicant must give a briefing before each takeoff and landing. If the operator, aircraft manufacturer, or training provider has not specified a briefing, the briefing must cover the items appropriate for the conditions, such as: departure runway, departure procedure, power settings, speeds, abnormal or emergency procedures prior to or after reaching decision speed (i.e., V_1 or V_{MC}), emergency return intentions, go-around/rejected landing procedures, initial rate of descent, and what is expected of the other crewmembers during the takeoff and landing. For single-pilot operations, the evaluator should request that the applicant verbalize the briefings. If the first takeoff and landing briefings are satisfactory, the evaluator may allow the applicant to brief only the changes, during the remainder of the evaluation.

Task A. Normal Takeoff and Climb

A normal takeoff begins from a standing or rolling start (not from a touch-and-go) with all engines operating normally during the takeoff and initial climb phase. When the flight test is conducted in an airplane, evaluators may have very little control over existing meteorological, airport, and traffic conditions. Evaluators are expected to make a reasonable attempt to evaluate a takeoff on a runway not favorably aligned with the prevailing wind. It will frequently be necessary, however, to evaluate this event with the crosswind component that exists on the active runway.

For takeoffs evaluated in a FFS, the crosswind component entered in the instructor operating station (IOS) should be between 10 and 15 knots. Occasionally, however, the crosswind components should be in excess of 15 knots, but must not exceed the crosswind component allowed by the operator's aircraft operating manual, or the maximum demonstrated value given in the approved Airplane Flight Manual (AFM).

Task B. Normal Approach and Landing

At least one of the required landings should be manually controlled with a crosswind. When the flight test is conducted in an airplane, evaluators may have very little control over existing meteorological, airport, and traffic conditions. Evaluators are expected to make a reasonable attempt to evaluate a landing on a runway not favorably aligned with the prevailing wind. It will frequently be necessary, however, to evaluate this event with the crosswind component that exists on the active runway.

For landings evaluated in a FFS, the crosswind component entered in the instructor operating station (IOS) should be between 10 and 15 knots. Occasionally, however, the crosswind components should be in excess of 15 knots, but must not exceed the crosswind component allowed by the operator's aircraft operating manual, or the maximum demonstrated value given in the approved Airplane Flight Manual (AFM).

Task G. Confined-Area Takeoff and Maximum Performance Climb (ASES, AMES)

This Task simulates a takeoff from an area that would require a takeoff and spiral climb; or a straight-ahead takeoff and climb from a narrow waterway with obstructions at either end. The evaluator must assess both takeoff situations for this Task.

In multiengine seaplanes with V_X values within 5 knots of V_{MC}, the use of V_Y or the manufacturer's recommendation may be more appropriate for this demonstration.

Task H. Confined-Area Approach and Landing (ASES, AMES)

This Task simulates an approach and landing to a small pond, which would require a spiral approach, wings level landing, and step turn upon landing; and a straight ahead approach and landing to a narrow waterway with obstructions at either end. The evaluator must evaluate both landing situations for this Task.

Task I. Rejected Takeoff

If completed in a multiengine airplane, the powerplant failure must be simulated before reaching 50 percent of V_{MC}.

Task J. Go-Around/Rejected Landing

The instrument conditions need not be simulated below 100 feet above the runway. This maneuver should be initiated approximately 50 feet above the runway or landing area and approximately over the runway threshold.

For those applicants seeking a VFR-only type rating and where this maneuver is accomplished with a simulated engine failure, it should not be initiated at speeds or altitudes below that recommended in the AFM/POH.

Completion of this Task may count for one of the three required actual landings. Wheel contact with the runway is not required.

IV. Inflight Maneuvers

Task A. Steep Turns

The applicant must demonstrate his or her ability to control the airplane manually without any intervention from the pilot monitoring, if applicable, or the evaluator. Use of available aircraft instrumentation is acceptable.

This task is to be conducted by reference to instruments. If IFR, the pilots should be situationally aware of location and any potential traffic.

For a VFR-only type rating, however, this Task will still be performed in visual conditions and the pilot should clear the area of traffic prior to beginning the maneuver; AA.IV.A.S3 would not be required to be by reference to instruments.

Task C. Specific Flight Characteristics

If the airplane does not have any specific flight characteristics identified in the FSB Report, this Task is not required.

V. Stall Prevention

The applicant must demonstrate his or her ability to control the aircraft without the intervention from the pilot monitoring, if applicable.

For Tasks A, B, and C, one must be induced while in a turn with a bank angle of 15-30 degrees; and, one should be induced by commands to the autopilot, if installed. In addition, these Tasks should be accomplished by reference to flight instruments. For a VFR only type rating, however, the tasks should be accomplished in visual conditions.

When conducted in the airplane, if a limitation of power application is necessary for operational considerations, the power should be set in accordance with the evaluator's instructions.

An impending stall means the same as an approach-to-stall or the first indication of a stall. As noted in AC 120-109A, an impending stall occurs when the angle of attack causes a stall warning. In accordance with aircraft certification standards[5], a stall warning must be furnished by inherent aerodynamics (e.g., buffet) or an acceptable stall warning device (e.g., stick shaker). The intent of the task is evaluate recognition of the stall warning and execution of the proper stall recovery procedure. Visual or aural messages do not meet the definition of a stall warning and cannot be used as indication of an impending stall for completion of these stall tasks.

Evaluation criteria for a recovery from an impending stall must not mandate a predetermined value for altitude loss and must not mandate maintaining altitude during recovery. Valid evaluation criteria must take into account the multitude of external (such as density altitude) and internal variables (i.e., airplane mass, drag configuration and powerplant response time) which affect the recovery altitude.

Reference the airplane flight manual or FSB Report, if available, for any aircraft-specific considerations concerning stalls.

VI. Instrument Procedures

Briefings

Each applicant must give a briefing before each takeoff/departure and approach/landing. If the operator, aircraft manufacturer, or training provider has not specified a briefing, the briefing must cover the items appropriate for the conditions, such as: departing/landing runway, departure/arrival procedure, instrument approach procedure, power settings, speeds, missed approach procedures, final approach fix, altitude at final approach fix, initial rate of descent, DA/DH/MDA, time to missed approach, and what is expected of the other crewmembers during the approach/landing. For single-pilot operations, the evaluator should request that the applicant verbalize the briefings. If the first takeoff/departure and approach/landing briefings are satisfactory, the evaluator may allow the applicant to brief only the changes, during the remainder of the flight.

Stabilized Approach Criteria

A stabilized approach is one in which the pilot establishes and maintains a constant angle glide path towards a predetermined point on the landing surface. It is based on the pilot's judgment of certain visual clues and depends on the maintenance of a constant final descent airspeed and configuration.

---

[5] 14 CFR part 25, section 25.207(b) and part 23, section 23.207(b)

Use of RNAV (Area Navigation) System Using GPS

If the practical test is conducted in an airplane equipped with an approach-approved RNAV system or FSTD that is equipped to replicate an approved RNAV system, the applicant must demonstrate approach proficiency using that system. If the applicant has contracted for training in an approved course that includes RNAV training, and the airplane/FSTD has a properly installed and operable RNAV system, the applicant must demonstrate RNAV approach proficiency.

RNAV (GPS) Approaches with Localizer Performance with Vertical Guidance (LPV) Minimums

LPV minimums with a decision altitude (DA) greater than 300 feet height above touchdown (HAT) may be used to satisfy a nonprecision approach task. Due to the stability and quality of its glidepath and localizer-like lateral navigation characteristics, an RNAV (GPS) approach with LPV minimums can be used to demonstrate precision approach proficiency, and therefore be used for a precision approach task, if the DA is equal to or less than 300 feet HAT.

Vertical or Lateral Deviation Standard

The standard is to allow no more than a ¼-scale deflection of either the vertical or lateral deviation indications during the final approach. As markings on flight instruments vary, a ¼-scale deflection of either vertical or lateral guidance is deemed to occur when it is displaced ¼ of the distance that it may be deflected from the indication representing that the aircraft is on the correct flight path.

Task A. Instrument Takeoff

Instrument conditions must be encountered or simulated at or before reaching an altitude of 100 feet above airport elevation. In a full flight simulator (FFS), the visibility value should be set to no greater than ¼ mile. An applicant must be evaluated on the ability to control the airplane, including making the transition to instruments as visual cues deteriorate and on the planning of the transition to an instrument navigation environment.

Task D. Nonprecision Approaches

The evaluator will select nonprecision approaches representative of the type the applicant is likely to use. The choices must use at least two different types of navigational aids.

Examples of acceptable nonprecision approaches include: VOR, VOR/DME, LOC procedures on an ILS, LDA, RNAV (GPS) to LNAV, LNAV/VNAV or LPV line of minima as long as the LPV DA is greater than 300 feet HAT. The equipment must be installed and the database must be current and qualified to fly GPS-based approaches.

The applicant must accomplish at least two nonprecision approaches in simulated or actual instrument meteorological conditions.

- One must include a published course reversal maneuver (e.g., procedure turn or Hold-in-Lieu). If a GPS-based approach is used to meet this requirement, the applicant must fly the course reversal maneuver on a published RNAV (GPS) approach procedure or a published Terminal Arrival Area (TAA) procedure.

- At least one must be flown without the use of an autopilot and without the assistance of radar vectors from the procedure's Initial Approach Fix; and the manually flown segment will begin no later than the FAF. The yaw damper and flight director are not considered parts of the autopilot for purposes of this Task.

- One should be flown with reference to backup or partial panel instrumentation or navigation display, depending on the aircraft's instrument avionics configuration, representing the failure mode(s) most realistic for the equipment used.

The evaluator has the discretion to have the applicant perform a landing or missed approach at the completion of each nonprecision approach.

Task E. Precision Approaches

The applicant must accomplish at least two precision approaches in simulated or actual instrument meteorological conditions to the decision altitude (DA) using aircraft navigational equipment for centerline and vertical guidance.

Acceptable instrument approaches for this part of the practical test are the ILS and GLS. In addition, if the installed equipment and database is current and qualified for RNAV (GPS) approaches to LPV minima, such an approach may be flown to demonstrate precision approach proficiency if the LPV DA is equal to or less than 300 feet HAT. RNAV (RNP) Instrument Approach procedures with RNP lines of minima of RNP 0.30 or less require specialized advanced training and equipment, and prior FAA authorization. Approved training programs that incorporate RNAV (RNP) procedures may utilize these special procedures in lieu of one of the precision approach procedures required.

- At least one must be flown without the use of an autopilot and the manually flown segment will begin no later than the FAF. Manually flown precision approaches may use raw data displays or may be flight director or heads-up-display (HUD) assisted, at the discretion of the evaluator.

- One should be flown with reference to backup or partial panel instrumentation or navigation display, depending on the aircraft's instrument avionics configuration, representing the failure mode(s) most realistic for the equipment used.

- At least one approach may be flown via the autopilot, if equipped, and if the DA/DH does not violate the authorized minimum altitude for autopilot operation.

The evaluator has the discretion to have the applicant perform a landing or missed approach at the completion of each precision approach.

Task F. Landing from a Precision Approach

For evaluations conducted in an airplane, if the applicant has flown the approach to a point where a safe landing and a full stop could have been made but circumstances beyond the control of the applicant prevented an actual landing, the evaluator may give credit for this Task. Credit may also be given for either Task I. Missed Approach or Area of Operation III, Task J. Go-Around/Rejected Landing, provided the applicable Task criteria is met.

Task G. Circling Approach

The approach and landing scenario must include visual maneuvering from the final approach course to a base or downwind leg, as appropriate, for the landing runway. The applicant may circle to land on a runway that is less than 90-degrees offset from the final approach course provided the applicant makes at least 90 degrees of total heading change(s).

Refer to Appendix 5: Practical Test Roles, Responsibilities, and Outcomes, Circle-to-Land Limitation on an ATP Certificate or Type Rating, for additional information regarding adding or removing this limitation.

Task H. Landing from a Circling Approach

For evaluations conducted in an airplane, if the applicant has flown the approach to a point where a safe landing and a full stop could have been made but circumstances beyond the control of the applicant prevented an actual landing, the evaluator may give credit for this Task. Credit may also be given for either Task I. Missed Approach or Area of Operation III, Task J. Go-Around/Rejected Landing, provided the applicable Task criteria is met.

Refer to Appendix 5: Practical Test Roles, Responsibilities, and Outcomes, Circle-to-Land Limitation on an ATP Certificate or Type Rating, for additional information regarding adding or removing this limitation.

Task I. Missed Approaches

The applicant must perform two missed approaches with one being from a precision approach.

One complete published missed approach must be accomplished. Additionally, in multiengine airplanes, a missed approach must be accomplished with one engine inoperative (or simulated inoperative). The engine failure may be experienced any time prior to the initiation of the approach, during the approach, or during the transition to the missed approach attitude and configuration.

Descending below the MDA or continuing a precision approach below DH/DA as appropriate, unless the runway environment is in sight is considered unsatisfactory performance. However, even if the missed approach is properly initiated at DA/DH, most airplanes descend below DA/DH because of the momentum of the airplane transitioning from a stabilized approach to a missed approach. This descent below DA/DH is not considered unsatisfactory, as long as the precision approach was not continued below DA/DH.

VII. Emergency Operations

Task B. Powerplant Failure during Takeoff

In a multiengine airplane certificated with V_1, V_R, or V_2 speeds, the failure of the most critical powerplant should be simulated at a point:

- after V_1 and prior to V_2, if in the opinion of the evaluator, it is appropriate under the prevailing conditions; or

- as close as possible after V_1 when V_1 and V_2 or V_1 and V_R are identical.

In a multiengine airplane certificated without V_1, V_R, or V_2 speeds, the failure of the most critical powerplant should be simulated at a point after reaching a minimum of V_{SSE}. If accomplished in the aircraft, the simulated powerplant failure should not be introduced at an altitude lower than 400 feet AGL. The evaluator should consider local atmospheric conditions, terrain, and aircraft performance available when determining when to introduce the simulated powerplant failure. In an FSTD there is no minimum altitude for introducing the powerplant failure.

If a powerplant failure (simulated if in the airplane) occurs after becoming airborne and before reaching an altitude where a safe turn can be made (ASEL, ASES) or the performance capabilities and operating limitations of the airplane will not allow the climb to continue (AMEL, AMES) the applicant should establish a power-off descent approximately straight-ahead.

For a 14 CFR part 25 or 14 CFR part 23, section 23.3(d) commuter multiengine airplane, if the (simulated) powerplant failure occurs at a point where the airplane can continue to a specified airspeed and altitude at the end of the runway commensurate with the airplane's performance capabilities and operating limitations, the takeoff should be continued. (AMEL, AMES)

If available, consult the FSB Report for any considerations in performing this task in the airplane.

Task C. Powerplant Failure (Simulated) (ASEL, ASES)

No simulated powerplant failure will be given by the evaluator in an airplane when an actual touchdown cannot be safely completed, should it become necessary.

Task D. Powerplant Failure and Restart Procedures (AMEL, AMES)

Refer to Appendix 6: Safety of Flight, Multiengine Airplane Considerations, for additional information concerning required airplane capabilities as they relate to this task. If the practical test is conducted in a multiengine airplane that requires the pilot to hold a type rating, the applicant may perform a simulated powerplant failure. In this case, a restart procedure must be considered for a given scenario and a simulated restart should be performed, if applicable to the airplane design and the given scenario.

When conducted in an FSTD, feathering or shutdown may be performed in conjunction with any Task and at locations and altitudes at the discretion of the evaluator.

Task E. Approach and Landing with a Powerplant Failure (Simulated) (AMEL, AMES)

For tests conducted in a propeller-driven airplane (other than those that require a type rating), the evaluator will set zero thrust after the applicant has simulated feathering the propeller following a simulated powerplant failure. The applicant must then demonstrate at least one landing with a simulated feathered propeller with the powerplant set to zero thrust. For all other airplanes, follow the manufacturer's recommended procedures.

In airplanes with three powerplants, the applicant must follow a procedure (if approved by the manufacturer and the training program) that approximates the loss of two powerplants, the center and one outboard powerplant. In other multiengine airplanes, the applicant must follow a procedure, which simulates the loss of 50 percent of available powerplants, the loss being simulated on one side of the airplane.

Task F. Precision Approach (Manually Flown) with a Powerplant Failure (Simulated) (AMEL, AMES)

At least one must be flown without the use of an autopilot. The applicant should begin manually flying prior to the final approach segment. Manually flown precision approaches may use raw data displays or may be flight director assisted, at the discretion of the evaluator. The simulated powerplant failure should occur before initiating the final approach segment and continue to a landing or a missed approach procedure, at the evaluator's discretion.

Task G. Landing from a No Flap or a Nonstandard Flap Approach

This task is required unless an airplane FSB Report has indicated otherwise; or the FAA Aircraft Evaluation Division has determined it is not required. The evaluator must determine whether checking on slats only and partial-flap approaches are necessary for the practical test. However, probability of asymmetrical flap failures should be considered in this making this determination.

Appendix 8: Use of Flight Simulation Training Devices (FSTD) and Aviation Training Devices (ATD): Airplane Single-Engine, Multiengine Land and Sea

Use of FSTDs

Title 14 of the Code of Federal Regulations (14 CFR) part 61, section 61.4, *Qualification and approval of flight simulators and flight training devices*, states in paragraph (a) that each full flight simulator (FFS) and flight training device (FTD) used for training, and for which an airman is to receive credit to satisfy any training, testing, or checking requirement under this chapter, must be qualified and approved by the Administrator for—

    (1) The training, testing, and checking for which it is used;

    (2) Each particular maneuver, procedure, or crewmember function performed; and

    (3) The representation of the specific category and class of aircraft, type of aircraft, particular variation within the type of aircraft, or set of aircraft for certain flight training devices.

14 CFR part 60 prescribes the rules governing the initial and continuing qualification and use of all FSTDs used for meeting training, evaluation, or flight experience requirements for flight crewmember certification or qualification.

An FSTD is defined in 14 CFR part 60 as an FFS or FTD:

    Full Flight Simulator (FFS)—*a replica of a specific type, make, model, or series aircraft. It includes the equipment and computer programs necessary to represent aircraft operations in ground and flight conditions, a visual system providing an out-of-the-flight deck view, a system that provides cues at least equivalent to those of a three-degree-of-freedom motion system, and has the full range of capabilities of the systems installed in the device as described in part 60 of this chapter and the QPS for a specific FFS qualification level. (part 1)*

    Flight Training Device (FTD)—*a replica of aircraft instruments, equipment, panels, and controls in an open flight deck area or an enclosed aircraft flight deck replica. It includes the equipment and computer programs necessary to represent aircraft (or set of aircraft) operations in ground and flight conditions having the full range of capabilities of the systems installed in the device as described in part 60 of this chapter and the qualification performance standard (QPS) for a specific FTD qualification level. (part 1)*

The FAA National Simulator Program (NSP) qualifies Level A-D FFSs and Level 4 – 7[6] FTDs. In addition, each operational rule part identifies additional requirements for the approval and use of FSTDs in a training program[7]. Use of an FSTD for the completion of the ATP – airplane practical test is permitted only when accomplished in accordance with an FAA approved curriculum or training program.

Use of ATDs

14 CFR part 61, section 61.4(c) states the Administrator may approve a device other than an FFS or FTD for specific purposes. Under this authority, the FAA's General Aviation and Commercial Division provides approval for aviation training devices (ATD).

Advisory Circular (AC) 61-136 (as amended), FAA Approval of Aviation Training Devices and Their Use for Training and Experience, provides information and guidance for the required function, performance, and effective

---

[6] The FSTD qualification standards in effect prior to part 60 defined a Level 7 FTD for airplanes (see Advisory Circular 120-45A, Airplane Flight Training Device Qualification, 1992). This device required high fidelity, airplane specific aerodynamic and flight control models similar to a Level D FFS, but did not require a motion cueing system or visual display system. In accordance with the "grandfather rights" of part 60, section 60.17, these previously qualified devices will retain their qualification basis as long as they continue to meet the standards under which they were originally qualified. There is only one Level 7 FTD with grandfather rights that remains in the U.S. As a result of changes to part 60 that were published in the Federal Register in March 2016, the airplane Level 7 FTD was reinstated with updated evaluation standards. The new Level 7 FTD will require a visual display system for qualification. The minimum qualified Tasks for the Level 7 FTD are described in Table B1B of Appendix B of part 60.

[7] 14 CFR part 121, section 121.407; part 135, section 135.335; part 141, section 141.41; and part 142, section 142.59.

use of ATDs for pilot training and aeronautical experience (including currency). FAA issues a letter of authorization (LOA) to an ATD manufacturer approving an ATD as a basic aviation training device (BATD) or an advanced aviation training device (AATD). The LOA will be valid for a 5-year period with a specific expiration date and include the amount of credit a pilot may take for training and experience.

> ***Aviation Training Device (ATD)***—*a training device, other than an FFS or FTD, that has been evaluated, qualified, and approved by the Administrator. In general, this includes a replica of aircraft instruments, equipment, panels, and controls in an open flight deck area or an enclosed aircraft cockpit. It includes the hardware and software necessary to represent a category and class of aircraft (or set of aircraft) operations in ground and flight conditions having the appropriate range of capabilities and systems installed in the device as described within the AC for the specific basic or advanced qualification level.*

> ***Basic Aviation Training Device (BATD)***—*provides an adequate training platform for both procedural and operational performance tasks specific to instrument experience and the ground and flight training requirements for the private pilot certificate and instrument rating per 14 CFR parts 61 and 141.*

> ***Advanced Aviation Training Device (AATD)***—*provides an adequate training platform for both procedural and operational performance tasks specific to the ground and flight training requirements for the private pilot certificate, instrument rating, commercial pilot certificate, airline transport pilot (ATP) certificate, and flight instructor certificate per 14 CFR parts 61 and 141. It also provides an adequate platform for tasks required for instrument experience and the instrument proficiency check.*

Note: *ATDs cannot be used for practical tests, aircraft type specific training, or for an aircraft type rating; therefore the use of an ATD for the ATP – Airplane practical test is not permitted.*

Credit for Time in an FSTD

14 CFR part 61, section 61.159 and 61.160 specify the minimum aeronautical experience requirements for a person applying for an ATP certificate. Paragraph (a)(6) of this section specifies the amount of credit a pilot can take towards the total time in an FFS or FTD as part of an approved training course in parts 121, 135, 141[8], or 142. Section 61.159 also provides allowances for crediting time in an FSTD towards time in class and instrument time. Credit may only be taken for time in a FFS towards time in class for multiengine airplanes; time in a FTD may not be used.

Credit for Time in an ATD

14 CFR part 61, section 61.159 and 61.160 specify the minimum aeronautical experience requirements for a person applying for an ATP certificate. In order to credit the time, the ATD must be FAA-approved and the time must be provided by an authorized instructor. AC 61-136 (as amended), states the LOA for each approved ATD will indicate the credit allowances for pilot training and experience, as provided under parts 61 and 141. Time with an instructor in an AATD may be credited towards the aeronautical experience requirements for the ATP certificate as specified in the LOA for the device used. Time in a BATD cannot be used for the ATP certificate. Time in an ATD cannot be used for credit towards the required time in class either. It is recommended that applicants who intend to take credit for time in an AATD towards the aeronautical experience requirements for the ATP certificate obtain a copy of the LOA for each device used so they have a record for how much credit may be taken. For additional information on the logging of ATD time reference AC 61-136 (as amended).

Use of an FSTD on a Practical Test

14 CFR part 61, section 61.45 specifies the required aircraft and equipment that must be provided for a practical test unless permitted to use an FFS or FTD for the flight portion. 14 CFR part 61, section 61.64 provides the criteria for using an FSTD for a practical test. Specifically, paragraph (a) states:

> *If an applicant for a certificate or rating uses a flight simulator or flight training device for training or any portion of the practical test, the flight simulator and flight training device—*

> > *(1) Must represent the category, class, and type (if a type rating is applicable) for the rating sought; and*

---

[8] As part of program approval, part 141 training providers must also adhere to the requirements for permitted time in an FFS or FTD per Appendices E or K to Part 141, as appropriate to the course of training.

> (2) *Must be qualified and approved by the Administrator and used in accordance with an approved course of training under part 141 or part 142 of this chapter; or under part 121 or part 135 of this chapter, provided the applicant is a pilot employee of that air carrier operator.*

Therefore, practical tests or portions thereof, when accomplished in an FSTD, may only be conducted by FAA aviation safety inspectors (ASI), aircrew program designees (APD) authorized to conduct such tests in FSTDs in 14 CFR parts 121 or 135, qualified personnel or designees authorized to conduct such tests in FSTDs for 14 CFR part 141 pilot school graduates, or appropriately authorized 14 CFR part 142 Training Center Evaluators (TCE).

In addition, 14 CFR part 61, section 61.64(b) states if an airplane is not used during the practical test for a type rating for a turbojet airplane (except for preflight inspection), an applicant must accomplish the entire practical test in a Level C or higher FFS and the applicant must meet the specific experience criteria listed. If the experience criteria cannot be met, the applicant can either—

> (f)(1) *[...] complete the following tasks on the practical test in an aircraft appropriate to category, class, and type for the rating sought: Preflight inspection, normal takeoff, normal instrument landing system approach, missed approach, and normal landing; or*

> (f)(2) *The applicant's pilot certificate will be issued with a limitation that states: "The [name of the additional type rating] is subject to pilot in command limitations," and the applicant is restricted from serving as pilot in command in an aircraft of that type.*

When flight Tasks are accomplished in an airplane, certain Task elements may be accomplished through "simulated" actions in the interest of safety and practicality. However, when accomplished in an FFS or FTD, these same actions would not be "simulated." For example, when in an airplane, a simulated engine fire may be addressed by retarding the throttle to idle, simulating the shutdown of the engine, simulating the discharge of the fire suppression agent, if applicable, and simulating the disconnection of associated electrical, hydraulic, and pneumatics systems. However, when the same emergency condition is addressed in a FSTD, all Task elements must be accomplished as would be expected under actual circumstances.

Similarly, safety of flight precautions taken in the airplane for the accomplishment of a specific maneuver or procedure (such as limiting altitude in an approach to stall or setting maximum airspeed for an engine failure expected to result in a rejected takeoff) need not be taken when a FSTD is used. It is important to understand that, whether accomplished in an airplane or FSTD, all Tasks and elements for each maneuver or procedure shall have the same performance standards applied equally for determination of overall satisfactory performance.

Appendix 9: References

This ACS is based on the following 14 CFR parts, FAA guidance documents, manufacturer's publications, and other documents.

Reference	Title
14 CFR part 1	Definitions and Abbreviations
14 CFR part 61	Certification: Pilots, Flight Instructors, and Ground Instructors
14 CFR part 91	General Operating and Flight Rules
14 CFR part 117	Flight and Duty Limitations and Rest Requirements: Flightcrew Members
14 CFR part 121	Domestic, Flag, and Supplemental Operations
14 CFR part 135	Requirements for Commuter and On Demand Operations
14 CFR part 142	Training Centers
49 CFR part 830	Notification and Reporting of Aircraft Accidents, or Incidents and Overdue Aircraft
AC 00-6	Aviation Weather
AC 00-30	Clear Air Turbulence Avoidance
AC 00-45	Aviation Weather Services
AC 00-46	Aviation Safety Reporting (Program) System (ASRP/ASRS)
AC 00-54	Pilot Windshear Guide
AC 20-117	Hazards Following Ground Deicing and Ground Operations in Conditions Conducive to Aircraft Icing
AC 60-28	FAA English Language Standard for an FAA Certificate Issued Under 14 CFR Parts 61, 63, 65, and 107
AC 61-67	Stall and Spin Awareness Training
AC 61-107	Aircraft Operations at Altitudes Above 25,000 Feet Mean Sea Level or Mach Numbers Greater Than .75
AC 61-136	FAA Approval of Aviation Training Devices and Their Use for Training and Experience
AC 61-138	Airline Transport Pilot Certification Training Program
AC 90-100	U.S Terminal and En Route Area Navigation (RNAV) Operations
AC 90-117	Data Link Communications
AC 91.21-1	Use of Portable Electronic Devices Aboard Aircraft
AC 91-74	Pilot Guide: Flight in Icing Conditions
AC 91-78	Use of Class 1 or Class 2 Electronic Flight Bag (EFB)
AC 91-79	Mitigating the Risks of a Runway Overrun Upon Landing
AC 120-27	Aircraft Weight and Balance Control
AC 120-51	Crew Resource Management Training
AC 120-57	Surface Movement Guidance and Control System
AC 120-58	Pilot Guide Large Aircraft Ground Deicing
AC 120-60	Ground Deicing and Anti-icing Program
AC 120-66	Aviation Safety Action Program (ASAP)
AC 120-74	Parts 91, 121, 125, and 135 Flightcrew Procedures During Taxi Operations
AC 120-76	Authorization for Use of Electronic Flight Bags
AC 120-82	Flight Operational Quality Assurance (FOQA)
AC 120-90	Line Operations Safety Audit (LOSA)
AC 120-100	Basics of Aviation Fatigue
AC 120-101	Part 121 Air Carrier Operational Control
AC 120-108	Continuous Descent Final Approach
AC 120-109	Stall Prevention and Recovery Training
AC 120-111	Upset Prevention and Recovery Training

Reference	Title
AC 135-17	Pilot Guide – Small Aircraft Ground Deicing
AIM	Aeronautical Information Manual
FAA-H-8083-1	Aircraft Weight and Balance Handbook
FAA-H-8083-2	Risk Management Handbook
FAA-H-8083-3	Airplane Flying Handbook
FAA-H-8083-6	Advanced Avionics Handbook
FAA-H-8083-15	Instrument Flying Handbook
FAA-H-8083-16	Instrument Procedures Handbook
FAA-H-8083-23	Seaplane, Skiplane, and Float/Ski Equipped Helicopter Operations Handbook
FAA-H-8083-25	Pilot's Handbook of Aeronautical Knowledge
FMSPs	Flight Management System Procedures
FSB Report	Flight Standardization Board Report (if available)
TPP	Terminal Procedures Publication
POH/AFM	Pilot's Operating Handbook/FAA-Approved Airplane Flight Manual
NOTAMs	Notices to Airmen
SAFO 17010	Incorrect Airport Surface Approaches and Landings
SAFO 19001	Landing Performance Assessments at Time of Arrival
STARs	Standard Terminal Arrival Routes
Other	Chart Supplements
	Enroute Low and High Altitude Charts
	Profile Descent Charts
	USCG Navigation Rules, International-Inland

Note: *Users should reference the current edition of the reference documents listed above. The current edition of all FAA publications can be found at www.faa.gov.*

Appendix 10: Abbreviations and Acronyms

The following abbreviations and acronyms are used in the ACS.

Abb./Acronym	Definition
14 CFR	Title 14 of the Code of Federal Regulations
AATD	Advanced Aviation Training Device
AC	Advisory Circular
ACS	Airman Certification Standards
ADM	Aeronautical Decision-Making
AELS	Aviation English Language Standard
AFM	Aircraft Flight Manual
AGL	Above Ground Level
AIM	Aeronautical Information Manual
AMEL	Airplane Multiengine Land
AMES	Airplane Multiengine Sea
APU	Auxiliary Power Unit
ASEL	Airplane Single-engine Land
ASES	Airplane Single-engine Sea
ASI	Aviation Safety Inspector
ATC	Air Traffic Control
ATD	Aviation Training Device
ATP	Airline Transport Pilot
BATD	Basic Aviation Training Device
CDI	Course Deviation Indicator
CDL	Configuration Deviation List
CRM	Crew Resource Management
CTP	Certification Training Program
DA	Decision Altitude
DH	Decision Height
DP	Departure Procedures
DPE	Designated Pilot Examiner
ELT	Emergency Locator Transmitter
FAA	Federal Aviation Administration
FFS	Full Flight Simulator
FMS	Flight Management System
FS	Flight Standards Service
FSB	Flight Standardization Board
FSTD	Flight Simulation Training Device
FTD	Flight Training Device
GBAS	Ground Based Augmentation System
GNSS	Global Navigation Satellite System

Abb./Acronym	Definition
GPS	Global Positioning System
HAT	Height Above Touchdown
IFR	Instrument Flight Rules
ILS	Instrument Landing System
IMC	Instrument Meteorological Conditions
LAHSO	Land and Hold Short Operations
LDA	Localizer-Type Directional Aid
LOA	Letter of Authorization
LOC	ILS Localizer
LPV	Localizer Performance with Vertical Guidance
MAP	Missed Approach Point
MEL	Minimum Equipment List
MFD	Multi-Function Display
NAS	National Airspace System
NOTAMs	Notices to Airmen
NSP	National Simulator Program
ODP	Obstacle Departure Procedure
PIC	Pilot-in-Command
POA	Plan of Action
POH	Pilot's Operating Handbook
PTS	Practical Test Standards
QPS	Qualification Performance Standard
RCAM	Runway Condition Assessment Matrix
RH	Rotorcraft-Helicopter
RNAV	Area Navigation
RNP	Required Navigation Performance
SAE	Specialty Aircraft Examiner
SID	Standard Instrument Departure
SMS	Safety Management System
SOP	Standard Operating Procedures
SRM	Single Pilot Resource Management
TPP	Terminal Procedures Publication
USCG	United States Coast Guard
VCOA	Visual Climb over the Airport
VFR	Visual Flight Rules
VMC	Visual Meteorological Conditions
VOR	Very High Frequency Omnidirectional Range
V_1	The maximum speed in the takeoff at which the pilot must take the first action (e.g., apply brakes, reduce thrust, deploy speed brakes) to stop the airplane within the accelerate-stop distance. V_1 also means the minimum speed in the takeoff, following a failure of the critical engine at V_{EF}, at which the pilot can continue the takeoff and achieve the required height above the takeoff surface within the takeoff distance.

Abb./Acronym	Definition
V_2	Takeoff safety speed
V_{MC}	Minimum control speed with critical engine inoperative
V_{MCG}	Minimum control speed on the ground with the critical engine inoperative
V_R	Rotation speed
V_{SSE}	Safe, intentional one-engine-inoperative speed. Originally known as safe single-engine speed
V_X	Best angle of climb speed
V_{XSE}	Best angle of climb speed with one engine inoperative
V_Y	Best rate of climb speed

Made in the USA
Columbia, SC
25 May 2019